b.o.n.d.a.g.e

b.o.n.d.a.g.e

A Memoir

Shaquenia Witherspoon

The woman who rescued me.
The woman who loved me unconditionally.
The woman who introduced me to the God inside.
The woman to whom I owe my life...

Mother Eugene Irving
Our flame burns eternal
I love you my Granny, my Mommy and Best
Friend

You are the promise!

Through you, the lineage changes.
Born in sin, out of evil and despair, cursed, abused,
rejected.
But raised up, rescued by God.

Given life, voice, love.

You are the promise!

~God

INTRODUCTION

I began this memoir over ten years ago on a quest to heal my mind and my heart so that I could breathe. That's all I wanted to do. Take one deep, uninhibited breath, and then another. Life for me has been a myriad of experiences that all seemed to culminate in pain. I've suffered major loss and endured years of betrayal. I've made bad decisions and plenty of mistakes. But like Miss Celie said, I'm here.

I truly believe that I'm still here for a reason. That my story is not just for me, but for the millions of people who hide inside of their stories because they feel there is no alternative. I have to believe that freeing myself will open the door for others to be freed. Others like men, bound by anger and defeat, struggling to regain their rightful roles in their homes and their communities. Others like women, bound by abuse and pain, living an endless cycle of fear, fueled by the very pain that bound them in the first place. Others like children, bound by generational chains they don't even understand, all the while emulating the behaviors of the parents they claim to hate.

We have allowed ourselves to be stripped from our rightful roles. We are bound, and there can be no healing until we are free.

The childhood sections of this story are based on my early memories. In some instances, I've asked family to fill in some blanks, but for the most part, I wrote it the way I remembered. I also know there are pockets and holes in my memories; places where the little girl me blocked out entire experiences. I have tried to ensure those places are also identified.

My purpose in writing this book is to affect change, not to villainize or hurt anyone. This book takes you through a journey of my life and because these experiences belong to me, it is not my intent to create confusion, distress or complicate anyone's life. My sharing these events begins the healing process, one which builds a bridge from pain and anger to love and acceptance.

This book is intended to help you BREATHE, because once you take that first free and clear breath, everything around you comes back into focus. Once you move past the fear of breathing deeply, God can blow His breath of life into your lungs. Once you decide that the shallow breaths you've been living on are no longer enough to sustain you; in that moment, the chains will fall, the pain will move, and you can walk out of betrayal, offense, neglect, disobedience, anger, grief and emotion:

b.o.n.d.a.g.e.

PROLOGUE

My earliest memory is of living in a house right off the water in Florida. My room had a sliding glass door that led to the beach and I loved to gaze out at the ocean. Maybe that is why to this day, water still has the massive ability to calm me. I couldn't have been more than three or four, my mother was in the Air Force, and I think we lived on base. I'm still not sure if these early memories are exact or just flashes of experiences that my toddler mind stitched together to create a patchwork quilt of my childhood life. But I know the water was real. And the sand...there was sand everywhere. I would often toddle out with my bucket and shovel and search for hidden treasures in the gritty, cool, crystal-like sand.

One day while thoroughly engrossed in my playing, a large crab crawled out the water. I have no idea when I noticed him, but I remember the fear that gripped my heart. My stomach dropped like I had just descended the hill of the world's highest roller coaster, and paralysis in my limbs kept me from moving even an inch away from the monster that threatened my very life. The sound of my blood-curdling scream would chill any mother to the bone and send her running, and my mother was no different. She came running to save me from the giant 'spider', calming me and soothing me as only a mother can. She held me in her arms, cooing gently in my ear. Making sure to hold in her laughter, understanding that her response to my reaction was the most important thing in the world to me. And she gave me what I needed. She lived up to my three-year-old expectations. She was my mother.

There are two life changing truths about this memory that have shaped me into the woman I am today. First, I have had arachnophobia ever since that day, still screaming, crying, and losing my breath whenever I see a spider. And second, that is the ONLY time in my life that my mother has run to my rescue.

PART ONE: QUEENIE

Just A Young Child

I was just a young child
With the ability to dream and be free
When all of my hopes and dreams
Were carelessly snatched from me
My hopes were deafened and cracked
By the sound of a killer whip
My dreams were smashed and killed
As the cord continuously hit
Then I was pulled out
And brought to what you call safety
Only to fall once again
Into the hands of the world and its gaiety
I was just a young child
Trying to regain my hopes and dreams
When a curious but ignorant question
Left again something to be snatched from me
This time it was more than just hopes and dreams
This time it was not my mother
For I had already lost her
You see, this time, it was my father
Torn from my daddy
For reasons I could not understand
I was told it was wrong, not right
To be touched by his hands
For 7 long years I hated
But not for the crime they said he committed
I hated my father because he left me
This, I felt, was the wicked
How could just a young child

Be put through such hurt and pain
Why couldn't I just live a happy life
A life without thunder and rain
Well, now I'm just past a young child
But the pain I then felt is still here
There seems to be no other way to let go
Except through all of my tears
One day I hope to reclaim
Those dreams from back a while
But it may not happen you see
Because I was just a young child

~Shaquenia Witherspoon-9th Grade~

CHAPTER 1

Any passerby could hear the screams loud and clear. But this was the eighties. Parents still whipped their kids back then. As a matter of fact, it was expected and deemed a necessary evil.

It was a beautiful fall day on the eastside of Detroit. The sun was shining brightly. The sky was a brilliant shade of blue, and the clouds were big, white, fluffy and looked good enough to eat. But for me, everything was spinning like a tornado. The wind was high, the world was dark, and I was dizzy and disoriented. Trying to figure out what had just happened...

"Shaquenia!" my mother screamed startling me from my sleep.

I jump up as she storms into my room. It is obvious that she is beyond angry, and my groggy brain is not awake enough to figure out what offense I could have committed while sleeping.

"Why aren't you dressed? Do you know what time it is?" she demands.

Now, to my six-year-old mind, this was a stupid question. We lived downstairs in a two family flat owned by my grandmother, who lived upstairs. Because my mother was such a hard sleeper, (due in part to the recreational drugs and alcohol she used daily), when she left in the morning, Granny would beat on our door to wake my mother and make sure she got me dressed for school.

"You...you didn't wake me up," I stuttered sleepily, rubbing my eyes.

"You heard Mama knock on the door. You knew it was time to get up. You just didn't wanna take your simple ass to school," she insisted.

"No I didn't Mommy--" but she wasn't listening.

"I should beat your ass!" with that, she spun on her heels and walked out of my room.

Scared to death now, I feel the tears rush to my eyes and down my cheeks. *How is it my fault? I didn't hear Granny knock. My room is way in the back of the house.* Before I could further contemplate if I was indeed in the wrong, my mother returned to my room with a belt in her hand. This is the belt that she wears with her long, gray dress. It is a wide, alligator skin belt, with a v-shaped middle, and a big buckle that fastens in the back.

I'm crying hard now, screaming, begging her not to whip me. Telling her I'm sorry. But she grabs me from the bed and

9

starts hitting me with the belt. I remember how it stung when it hit my skin. How I cried and squirmed and tried to get away. How she cursed and yelled, and beat me harder...

And now I'm trying to get dressed. Sniffling, body on fire, skin red and inflamed, and still confused about what I did wrong. I slid on a pair of cut-off denim shorts and reached for my shirt, a blue and white, flowered crop top with yellow blossoms on it. I had just pulled my shirt over my head when my mother's boyfriend, Dwayne, walked into my room. I didn't pay him any attention, especially since I was still trying to catch my breath and stop sniffling before my mother came back for another round. I heard him unplugging the light and something else in my room, but I thought nothing of it...until I felt something like fire whip across my back and spread like a fever. Unable to even scream out in pain at first, I spun around and saw Dwayne holding a big, thick, brown extension cord. Before I could process this, he raised his arm, dropped it down, and I felt that same fire across my shoulder. This time I did scream. Only this scream was worse than the spider scream. This scream spoke volumes. It said my life was in danger. It said he is hurting me. It said MOMMY!

But she didn't come. I screamed and screamed for her. Screamed as I got hit in my face, my stomach, my back. Screamed as I got hit on my arms and legs and feet. Screamed as every inch of my body burned like hot lava erupting from the Earth's oldest volcano. And when I looked up, I saw her. But she wasn't coming for me. She was standing outside my room, leaning on the refrigerator, with a coffee cup in her hand. Her head cocked to the side, with a look of sheer confusion on her face. Like she couldn't hear me. Like she couldn't see this man taking my childhood away with every stripe. Tearing my security away with every scream

she...just...stood...there...and watched...

I don't know if it was the fact that my screams had turned into strained, breathless whimpers, or the reality that my skinny body had swollen to three times its normal size, but a few minutes later, my mother sprang into action. She took in a sharp, frightened breath and ran into my room, grabbing him off of me. To this day, I believe it was less because she wanted to save me and more because she saw my beaten, bruised, swollen, discolored body, and was afraid she would get into trouble once Granny or someone else saw me. She left me on the floor of my room, where I was breathing raggedly and sobbing profusely, and went into the bathroom. I only knew this because I heard the water running in the bathtub. With a new-found sense of urgency, she ran back into my room, carried me into the bathroom, stripped off my clothes, and dumped me into a tub of ice cold water. This took away my last bit of breath. Once in the tub, I fought against her, but she told me that I had to stay in the water.

Beaten, spirit broken, and physically weak, I gave up, body shivering, and teeth chattering in the cold. My mother left the bathroom and came back with the ice trays from the freezer and a bottle I couldn't quite see. As if the water wasn't cold enough, she emptied all the ice trays into the tub with me. All I could do was cry silently now, no energy left to make a sound. Eyes closed, freezing, scared and exhausted, I remember wishing my Granny would come save me, and this made me cry even harder.

Suddenly, my already traumatized body started to burn. Not like the burn of the belt, or even the extension cord. This burn was different. The intensity of this heat gave me strength to once again try and fight my way out of the tub. This burn helped me find my screams. This burn was excruciating, and I thought I was going to die. My mother held me down by my shoulders, yelling over my screams that I had to stay in the water, that it would help. That the ice would help the swelling, and the liquid from the mysterious bottle would keep my open wounds from being infected. Alcohol. After being severely beaten, not once but twice, I was forced to sit in a tub of cold water, ice cubes, and alcohol. I wanted out. Why weren't my screams working? Why couldn't she see my tears? Why wouldn't she rescue me??

My memory of how the events following my beating transpired is foggy and pieced together mainly from my grandmother's account of the story. According to her, she hadn't seen me in almost a week. This was odd because she and I were very close, and I practically lived upstairs in her house. What she didn't know was that my mother was purposely keeping me away from her, hiding me out, trying to give me a chance to heal.

Granny said that one day I snuck upstairs while my mother was sleeping and knocked on her door. Glad to see me, she naturally folded me into her arms as only a grandmother can do for a great big hug. Immediately she noticed that I grimaced in pain and asked me what was wrong. She said that when I told her Dwayne had beat me, she lifted my shirt, and saw all of the bruises and marks on my upper body. Of course, she was livid. She called my Uncle Charles over to the house, and there was some type of confrontation with my mother. Dwayne fled the house because my uncle, obviously upset when he saw the damage done to me, was not at all in a talking mood, and Granny called protective services.

Granny moved me in upstairs with her while everything got sorted out. I don't know what my mother told my Granny about what happened to me, but whatever the story was, Granny wasn't buying it. Although Granny had always been protective of me because my mother conceived me at such a young age (fifteen), this most recent turn of events sealed our two paths in stone. Granny and I would never again be separated for any long amount of time. I didn't know it then, but she would become my best friend, my tireless supporter, as well as my greatest inspiration.

Going through this traumatic event at a such a young age, I'm sure I just wanted to forget as much of the pain as I could. Because of this, so many memories have blurred into others. Dates, times, periods...but there are certain occurrences that are stained in my brain like red dye. No matter how much I try to forget, no matter how I try to convince myself that they didn't happen, no matter how I try to cleanse myself of the slimy feeling these memories invoke, they just won't go away.

One of these memories happened shortly after Granny called protective services. We were all standing in the stairwell. My mother was standing in front of her door downstairs, Granny and I were on the steps in the middle, and the social worker for Child Protective Services was standing at the front door, along with another person; either a police officer, or another social worker. The grown-ups were talking, most of which I didn't understand. But all of a sudden, the social worker said something that made my ears perk up...

"Ms. Jackson, we will return your daughter to you if you agree to discontinue your relationship with Dwayne."

I looked up at my mother expectantly, because although I loved my Granny to death, this was my mother. We belonged together. She was teaching me how to wink, and I hadn't quite learned yet. I was her only child. She loved me. Right?

My mother looked at the social worker, and replied simply, "Go to hell."

There was a pregnant pause in which everyone took a moment to process what she said, and then the social worker looked at me with just a hint of pity and turned to my grandmother.

"Mrs. Irving, unless you take her, your granddaughter will become a ward of the state."

Glaring at my mother in disgust, Granny replied, "No blood of mine will be a ward of the state. She will stay here with me."

As if sensing the pain that attacked my heart in those moments, Granny grabbed my shoulder with her hand, squeezing hard, telling me silently that we were going to be okay. Transferring that grandmotherly brand of comfort that can never be duplicated. I just looked at my mother. Tears once again streaming down my face. Crying out to her, this time without words, begging her to pick me. Begging her to love me. Begging God to let me be enough, but I wasn't.

So, Granny got temporary custody, and that would lead to her taking care of me for the rest of her life.

CHAPTER 2

Granny was in her mid-fifties when she was awarded custody of me, having already raised five children of her own, but she never complained, or made me feel unwanted. She stepped right up to the plate and became everything I needed. After losing me to Granny, my mother's drug use spiraled out of control. She disappeared for months at a time. She would pop up out of the blue and tell Granny that she wanted to take me to the movies, or shopping, or on some trip. Granny would see that she was high, and tell her no. Mom would cuss her, calling her horrible names, even going so far as to break out the windows on both our car and house to show her anger and frustration. See, in my mother's eyes, Granny took me from her. Everyone had over reacted. I was never beaten, just simply given a whipping for misbehaving like every other black child would get. She believed that Granny stole custody of me, and then kept me from her just to punish her. I believe this is the story that she had to force herself to ingest to sleep at night. We went on like this for years. Her making and breaking promises, but always choosing a man, the world, and her drugs over being a mother to her only child.

In the meantime, Granny had to readjust her life to include me in it on a full-time basis. This was no easy feat as she worked crazy hours and was used to coming and going as she pleased. She knew she needed her job now more than ever if she was going to be able to support me, so she enlisted the help of my father and the other side of my family. The deal, if I remember correctly, was for me to live with my dad at my great-grandmother's house during the week, and Granny would come get me on the weekends, returning me to them after church on Sundays.

I was truly a Daddy's girl. I loved my Daddy just because he was my Daddy. And I clung to him because in my little girl mind, he was all I had left after losing my mother. He spoiled me, lavishing me with tons of affection, hugs and kisses. We lived in a house with my great-grandmother, and at any given time a number of others could be found with us: my uncle, my dad's younger brother, my paternal grandmother, my aunt, (who was really my grandmother's lover), my dad's girlfriend, and later, my newborn little brother.

For the most part, I remember laughing and playing and having a good time. I would wait every day for my uncle to come home from school or wherever, because I knew he'd have some chocolate Now-or-Later candies for me. He would walk in, and I would squeal and run into his arms, then he'd pick me up and throw me high into the air (he was about 6'4) and catch me, tickling me on the way down. When I could barely breathe from laughing so hard, he'd hug me tight, and give me my candy reward. I simply adored him.

There are some not so good memories though. I can remember sitting on the floor one day with a coloring book and some crayons. My grandmother, (dad's mom), was home this day, and she was in the living room with me. Besides my uncle, everyone else in the house smoked, so naturally, I placed a crayon between my fingers and pretended to be smoking it while I was coloring. At some point my grandmother noticed me and became furious.

"So, you wanna smoke, huh?" she asked.

Instantly afraid, I knew I had done something wrong because of the tone of her voice. I dropped the crayon and shook my head.

"Yeah, you wanna smoke." I watched as she grabbed the little purse that held her cigarettes, pulled one out, and lit it.

"Here, since you think you're grown enough to smoke, then smoke." she said as she held the cigarette out to me, smoke spiraling into the air in front of my nose.

Tears forming in my eyes, I shook my head again, and moved my face away from the smoke.

"I said take the damn cigarette and smoke it!" she yelled.

Scared to take the cigarette, but even more afraid of what she would do if I didn't, I placed the cigarette between my fingers as I had seen her and the other adults do so many times.

"I said smoke it!" she insisted.

Slowly, I put the smoking stick to my lips, puffed on it, and immediately blew the smoke right out of my mouth, grimacing at the horrible taste on my tongue.

"No! Inhale the smoke! You grown right? Smoke the damn cigarette, inhale it, and you better smoke the whole thing!"

With tears spilling down my cheeks, I puffed again, this time pulling deep into my asthmatic lungs. Instantly, I began to choke and cough, feeling a burn in my nose and throat that I thought would kill me. I tried to give the cigarette back to her, pleaded, told her I didn't want to smoke, would never smoke, but she was relentless. We sat there, me inhaling, coughing and choking, crying and begging, until the cigarette was gone.

"Now, I bet you'll keep your little grown ass in a child's place next time." she said as she lit herself another one.

I said nothing, but soon ran to the bathroom to throw up. For the majority of my life, just the smell of cigarette smoke could send me into a coughing fit and have me reaching for my inhaler. To this day, I have never smoked a cigarette. With the exception of burning a cigar for the smell, or a clove on occasion, that experience definitely had the desired effect.

CHAPTER 3

From what I can piece together, my dad had it pretty rough growing up. Watching his grandparents go back and forth fighting and shooting at each other; living in a neighborhood where he was constantly challenged and forced to defend himself and his baby brother; raised without a father in the home; and to top it all off, raised by a mother now identifying as a lesbian, who lived out her wild years in front of her children. My dad grew up fast and learned how to take care of himself.

I don't offer excuses for him, rather, I have grown enough in my own life to understand that there is a *reason* for everything. When a child is exposed to something without proper guidance, that child is left to process the experience based on his limited understanding. My father grew up surrounded by violence, drugs, alcohol and sex.

In order to understand where a person lands, you have to first understand where they began.

I must tell this portion of the story both from some of his perspective and some of mine. Like many of my memories, I have blocked a lot of details and dates, and only remember flashes of experiences.

While living with my mother, I had been exposed to her drug use and some sexual activities that I had no way of understanding, and definitely didn't need to see. It is important to understand that once those doors are opened in the mind of a child, there is no way to close them on her own. Without the proper tools to help me process what I had seen, all of this 'stuff' was just floating around in my brain.

My dad told me that one day I made a sexually suggestive statement that a seven-year-old girl shouldn't have been able to make (something about licking his nipples). He said that he began to question me, trying to figure out where I learned it, and how much I understood about what I'd said. Based on his account, one thing led to another, and everything got out of control.

Let me pause here. In no way do I justify what my father did to me. He betrayed my trust, he confused me in ways that it would take upwards of twenty years for me to unravel, and on some levels, he indirectly caused me to make some decisions in my life that have affected me for years. However, I also believe that my father was sick, and I'm not sure that he even knew it. How on earth can a child grow up like he did, see what he saw, experience what he experienced, and not be sick somehow? With no one to interpret those experiences, no one to help him process those feelings and thoughts the correct way, no one to guide him down the right path, there is no possible way he could come out unscathed.

Sexual demons are some of the hardest to overcome, and if you don't recognize them for what they are, they will ride you until you die. My father was riddled with sexual demons. He was not a bad person, and although he has never told me anything of the sort, I honestly believe that someone sexually abused him when he was a child. I could be wrong, but usually those demons ride deep. He may not even see the experience as abuse, but I truly believe it happened.

Because of all these mixed signals in his brain, there was nothing to stop my dad from going too far with me. If there were any warning signals, the adrenaline and feel good sensations were much more powerful than the risks, probably because he had been living in a world of risk his entire life.

My father never brutalized me. He never penetrated me. He never frightened, threatened, or beat me. In fact, he was so tender and loving, that I had no idea his touches and kisses were wrong. I had no clue that his bare chest was not for my head, that his nipples were not supposed to be licked by me. That the lessons he was teaching me were wrong for me to learn. At seven years old, my body was experiencing feelings that it was not ready for, but I was with my Daddy, my best friend, so I believed it was okay. It never crossed my mind that it could be wrong. Daddy told me that it was our little secret, he simply told me not to tell, and I obeyed because when your Dad tells you not to do something, you just don't do it.

Because my father and I are able to have a relationship today, one that a lot of people don't understand, and because I am the one who endured these things, it is very hard to discuss this in detail. But to be fair and accurate, and if I am to finally complete the last phase of this healing process, I know that I must also tell the hardest parts.

There are two instances that I somehow didn't black out with the others. I used to sleep on the couch in the living room of my great-grandmother's house. I remember waking up one night to the sound of my dad and his girlfriend having sex in his bedroom. I knew what they were doing because I had seen and heard my mother many times. I guess I had fallen back to sleep, because the next thing I remember was my dad on his knees at my ankles, lifting my nightgown. He was gently placing kisses on my legs, traveling up my thighs, pulling my panties down, and touching me...there. I remember thinking that I must be really special if he left her in their bed to come and see me...

I only have one memory where I remember feeling completely uncomfortable with my dad and wishing he would leave me alone. I was getting ready for school one morning, and my dad came in the room where I was getting dressed. He had on a white wife beater, and the black doo rag he was known for wearing, but was naked from the waist down, and was stroking himself. He walked up to me and grabbed my head, motioning for me to take him in my mouth. Up to this point, I had never told him no to the things he'd asked me to try, but for some reason, something in me didn't want to do this. He pouted, poked his lip out, and rubbed his penis on my lips. I remember that it was wet, with what I now know was pre-seminal fluid. It turned my stomach, but I was a daddy's girl, and I didn't want to disappoint him, so I opened my mouth. He took a sharp breath, and I could tell that made him happy. My eyes welled up with tears, but I held them in, not wanting to make him unhappy. Silently he directed me on how to please him, and I tried my best not to choke. At some point, it felt like he was growing in my mouth, although that didn't make sense to me, and then I felt something hot and salty squirt into my mouth. I had no idea what to do, so I just swallowed it to keep from choking. I will never forget the taste. Even now, I sometimes wake up in the middle of the night with that taste in my mouth.

I assume that by this point, things had grown to an out-of-control point. I don't know what would have happened, but I guess it's a good thing I never had to find out. Like most little girls my age, I had a group of friends at school, and we were chatty and secretive, silly and close. In the bathroom at school one day, one of the girls was sharing how she liked one of the little boys in our class and wanted to kiss him on the cheek or something. We laughed and giggled as little girls do. Somehow, I told the girls something that I had done with my dad. Again, in my head, I wasn't doing anything wrong, so it wasn't really a secret, I was just talking to my girls. Thankfully, one of the girls knew that this didn't sound right. She told our teacher, who informed the principal, who called Child Protective Services.

I remember them coming to my school that same day to speak to me. It's funny how the entire time I had been involved with my father, I never felt ashamed, or wrong. But as soon as they started questioning me, I knew. I cried, I was afraid, I was ashamed, I begged them not to tell my dad that I'd told. I didn't want him to be mad at me. Something inside of me instantly knew that it was all wrong, that my life would be forever changed. I felt dirty. And even through all of that, my greatest fear was that my dad would be mad at me, that he would stop loving me...just like my mother had.

They assured me that everything would be alright and sent me back to class. The rest of the day went by in a haze. I didn't say a word to anyone about what happened when I got home. I went through my normal afternoon and evening routine of homework and dinner. Sometime after dinner, I heard a knock on the door, and my heart fell into my stomach. I knew who it was before my great-grandmother even got up to answer it. I was scared to death, and I didn't move an inch. When she opened the door, I saw that outside there was an unmarked car, two police cars, and the social worker from earlier was standing on my porch with the officers that I assumed belonged to the police cars.

I became hysterical. As the social worker started to explain to Nanny (the name we called my great-grandmother) the reason for their presence, I cried uncontrollably, and found it hard to breathe. Nanny was instantly angered, of course, not believing that her grandson was capable of what they were suggesting, and she began to get loud. At the same time, the phone started ringing. Somehow, I knew it was my dad, who had earlier gone to visit friends who lived up the block, where I'm sure he could see all the commotion.

It all unfolded like a movie scene. The front of the house flickering from red to blue in the harsh glare of the police lights. The knocking on the door that sounded like boulders crashing into the house. The constant ringing of the phone, that played like a melody underneath Nanny's cursing and the calm rebuttals of the social worker. The beating of my heart bursting in my ears as I struggled to breathe, wishing for a place to hide, a way to make it all go away. Every nerve ending in my body was firing, screaming to me that life would never be the same again.

I answered the phone crying so hard that I could barely speak, and I remember telling my dad that I was sorry over and over. He assured me that everything was okay, that he wasn't mad at me, that everything was going to be fine. Still I cried. It felt like the weight of the world was on me at that very moment, and I cried harder than I'd ever cried in my life. I understood, right then, that I had just lost my father.

In a daze, I remember the social worker telling me to put some jeans underneath my gown and my purple corduroy robe. After a few more words with Nanny, they loaded me in the back of one of the squad cars and took me away. I don't know if my dad was arrested that night, or sometime after, but I do know that he was eventually arrested on charges of child molestation.

After stopping by Burger King to get me something to eat, I was taken to the precinct, where they called my Granny and informed her of the situation. She immediately came to get me.

It's amazing how much of my early childhood I've blocked, versus the things that I vividly remember. I can still see the look of shock, hurt, disgust and anger on my Granny's face when she got to the police station. Because I was so young, I assumed those feelings were all geared toward me. I dropped my head in shame, not knowing what to say. She spoke with the officers quietly, and because she had custody of me anyway, was allowed to take me home.

Granny didn't talk to me in the car. She didn't ask me any questions, and she wasn't at all mean. She was just quiet, except for the humming that she did whenever she was really stressed and needed to talk to God. I knew from experience that outwardly she was humming, but she was praying on the inside. I also knew that she only did this in dire situations, and that made me feel worse.

When we got to the house, Granny went to the kitchen, made a pot of coffee, and sat me at the table. She simply wanted to know why I hadn't told her what had been going on. How do you explain that you didn't tell because you didn't really know that you should? How do you say that you enjoyed being with your dad, loved the attention, loved that he loved you? How do you tell her that you looked forward to your time with him because he made you feel like the most special person in the world? That you only had one parent left and you didn't want to lose him too?

All I could do was cry.

Granny went on to explain to me that what my father had been doing was nasty and dirty. That he should be ashamed. That no father should ever do those dirty things to his child. That he was a dog. With every word she spoke, I felt smaller and smaller. Surely, if he was these things, then so was I. Surely, I must be dirty, and nasty. Surely, I should be ashamed of myself too. And I was. By the time she was done talking to me, I hated him. Hated him because I didn't know how not to love him. Hated him because he made me dirty.

Hated him because he let them take me away...but I hated myself more.

Somehow, I convinced myself that this was all my fault. There had to be something wrong with me. Why didn't I know it was wrong? Why wasn't I smarter? My friends knew, but I didn't. My Granny knew, but I didn't. What was wrong with me? Why did I keep making people stop loving me? I hated myself, and I hated him because everyone said that I should.

What hurt me most was the feeling I got that Granny blamed herself because she left me with him. She took me there every week. She delivered me into his hands. She asked herself how she couldn't know. Why I didn't trust her enough to tell her. She stayed up at night, trying to figure it all out. I heard her late at night, when she thought I was asleep, talking to my aunts. Heard her hurt, her pain, her fear, her insecurity. Heard the unspoken responsibility she placed on herself. And that hurt me most of all. Because I knew it wasn't her fault...it was mine. Granny was the strongest person I knew, and I had broken her. The coffee pot filled again and again because of me. The kitchen filled with the sound of her humming every morning because of me. She was hurting because of me.

It's funny the way the mind of a child works. During all this confusion, I also figured out something else. As hurt as Granny was, as disappointed as she seemed, she didn't leave me. As a matter of fact, each time that I needed her, she ran to my rescue. I had lost my mom, and I was losing my dad, but Granny remained a constant in my life. No matter what happened, what mistakes I made, how bad it got, she was there. Granny did what my parents were unable to do. She became for me what most children in my situation never receive, a safe place. A landing pad. Home. I believe I connected myself to her at this realization, and nothing would separate us ever again. For the rest of our time together, she was my everything.

Of course, once word of the molestation got out, it all went downhill. My uncles were pissed, my aunts were appalled, and my mother even showed up to clown. On the other side of the family, Nanny didn't believe me, my grandmother was angry, and my dad was in jail.

I'll never forget the day I had to testify at the sentencing hearing. We were in a room: the bailiff, the judge, my dad, his lawyer, Granny, a representative from CPS, and our lawyer. I looked everywhere but at my dad as they read off the case information and rattled off the charges. As they asked him questions, I averted my eyes. I just couldn't look at him. My stomach ached. My head hurt. I just wanted out of the room. Noticing my discomfort, the lawyer leaned down and asked me if I was okay. I nodded, but I wasn't okay. The judge called me to the stand so I could be questioned. This was the hardest thing in the world for me because now I was in front and looking away from my dad was much harder. They were asking me something, but I couldn't concentrate, my eyes were drawn to him, and I couldn't force my mouth to move.

I leaned over to the judge and asked him if they could take my dad out of the room because I was afraid with him there. The bailiff removed him, and the questioning proceeded. I don't remember what was said, just that I focused on Granny the whole time, and was so relieved when it was all over. My dad was sentenced to one year in prison, and ordered to have no contact with me, physical or otherwise, unless at some point I decided I wanted him to again be a part of my life.

I wouldn't see or talk to him again for another three years, when he would pop up at my fifth-grade graduation. I don't know what prompted him to break the rules, but he showed up with his wife and my two younger brothers. I was on the stage because I was being recognized for several achievements, and all of a sudden, the hairs on the back of my neck stood up. I looked to the back of the auditorium and saw him making his way to a seat. Immediately, I began to hyperventilate. I was scared to death. My mother, who was on one of her many 'drug-free' stints was at graduation with me because Granny had to work. She saw the change in me and started to frown, asking me what was wrong with her eyes. Following my stare, she turned and saw my father and his family.

Somehow, I made it through the graduation without having an asthma attack, and afterward, my dad approached us. I didn't really say much to him, but was ecstatic to see my younger brother, who was only one when I stopped having contact with that side of my family. There was also another brother that I had never met, who had been born after all the drama. Their mother was the girlfriend that lived with us back when I stayed with Nanny, and now she was his wife. I remember feeling weird, and not wanting him to touch me. I wasn't ready, and he didn't push me.

I didn't see him again until I was fourteen years old.

CHAPTER 4

Over the years, I always wanted to believe that my experiences no longer touched me. That the years of therapy, relentless church services and the abundance of love from my family had somehow healed me, and I was no longer affected by my past. I convinced myself that I was unscathed, that I had beaten the odds, that now everything was fine.

When I was nine or ten years old, I fell head over heels for a boy in my congregation, we'll call him 'James'. At fourteen or fifteen years old (I don't remember our exact ages), James was fascinating to me. He had a brilliant smile, nice lips, and unlike the other boys at church, he wasn't mean to me. He teased like boys do, laughing at me when I got in trouble, or pulling my ponytails, but he also told me I was pretty, he smiled at me, and his 'church hug' was different than everyone else's. That attention was all I needed.

Our congregation was intimate and built mostly of families. Everyone knew everyone, and all the youth were being raised the same. Bible study on Tuesday, Mission on Wednesday, Choir Rehearsal on Friday, any number of meetings on Saturday, and church all day on Sunday. Like it or not, growing up in the Baptist church back then, this was your life. We joke about how bad it was now, but we had tons of fun, and we spent almost all our free time together (we clearly didn't have a choice).

There were the plays and dramatic productions that we all starred in for Black History Month, Easter, Christmas and any other reason Granny could come up with, since most of them were written and/or directed by her. There were the trips they took us on to Frankenmuth, the skating rink, bowling, Boblo and just about anywhere else we asked to go. The picnics and cookouts we had outside the church. The concerts, revivals, conventions and other programs we had with the other churches in our district. They kept us together, and for the most part, they kept us out of trouble. When you heard of one of us gone awry, it could usually be traced back to a drop in church attendance. The elders would tsk, giving one of their long speeches on the importance of keeping God first in our lives, and suddenly we'd hear that kid's name called out in prayer meeting.

Once I realized that James 'liked' me, any complaining about going to these church events ceased on my part. I was always excited to go, knowing he would be there, and hoping I would get a couple of seconds alone to get a real hug. I saw him flirting with the older girls, but I knew this was just for show, at least, that's what I told myself. Eventually, a secret hug turned into a stolen kiss, and that stolen kiss, for me, equated to love.

Our church building was small and old. The sanctuary had brown wood paneled walls that were warped in places from years of being exposed to moisture. The sanctuary floors were covered in thin, threadbare red carpet, with black stripes that reflected the light. Uncomfortable wooden pews, with no padding, that made your butt numb when the preacher took too long. Fans hanging dangerously from the ceiling that only managed to blow hot air around on stifling summer days. Old fashioned steam radiators with chipped silver paint, hissing loudly in the corners on cold winter mornings, that would also burn a hole in your brand new white tights if you got too close. It wasn't fancy, but it was home.

The basement had always scared me, with its spider webs and musty smells, its shadows and mildewed corners, but when James told me to meet him in the furnace room, I never hesitated. The small dark room, filled with boxes and mice traps became our special place. He would kiss me, hold me, tell me that he loved me. He taught me how to French kiss, how to hold my head so that our noses wouldn't collide. I learned to hold my breath just right so that I didn't breathe on him too much, and how to make sure that my mouth wasn't too juicy, but just wet enough. I convinced myself that I was special, that out of all the girls he could have, he chose me. I mean, James was five years older than me and in high school, so I must be that deal, right?

Outside of the betrayal by my father, this is probably the first instance of my learning to become who someone else needed me to be in order to gain what I perceived as love; the first time I unconsciously pulled the mask on. I remember trying to be more mature, so James wouldn't think I was a silly little girl. My dad had already taught me how to keep a secret, so I played the game well in front of others. Inside, there was a feeling of control, that I was in charge of this love, and no one could take it away from me. I knew that to be loved, I couldn't tell anyone. Every time I told, love was snatched away from me, so I kept my mouth shut and enjoyed our stolen moments.

James never tried to push me in any other ways, and he never brought up sex. He had no way of knowing that his kisses, his gentle caresses on my leg, or the way he held me in his arms for a hug ignited those feelings from long ago. Those feelings that made me crave love and attention. Those feelings that convinced me all I had to do was oblige. Those feelings that taught me my body was the key to getting and keeping love.

In hindsight, I'm amazed that we got away with our little forbidden romance as long as we did. During one of the times when my mother was clean, and my grandmother was trying to help her by allowing her to stay with us, she went through my stuff and found my diary. My Aunt Madie had always encouraged me to read and write, and so I'd started journaling in elementary school. The diary that my mother found was a makeshift book I'd created using orange construction paper as the front and back covers, and sheets of blank paper cut in half all stapled together. I'd written in big bold letters on the front: FOR MY EYES ONLY.

Not only did my mother ignore my obviously well-constructed warning, she shared what she'd read with my grandmother. They called me into Granny's bedroom and I saw the book on the bed. My heart stopped beating and breathing became a chore. I began whizzing through my entries in my head. The one about how his tongue felt in my mouth. The one expressing my undying love and devotion to him. The one describing the chills I got whenever he touched me. The tears began to fall. The shame fell on my shoulders like torrents of rain. I couldn't look my grandmother in the eye. All those years ago she'd inadvertently taught me that love is shame. Love makes me dirty. Love makes me a dog. Yet, I didn't know how to stop chasing love.

My grandmother asked a lot of questions, and I realized that she was more concerned with the age difference than anything else. In all honesty, James and I hadn't done anything horrible, but I imagine this also catapulted her back to our shared shame, as she tried to figure out how this was happening again. I remember being so angry with my mother. It seemed that she was happy to have found something on me, something that tarnished me in Granny's sight. My mother had long ago started to compete with me for Granny's love and attention, and the resentment she had for me continued to build as Granny over and over chose me. It wasn't because she loved me more, or because she didn't love my mother; it was because my mother couldn't handle the responsibility of raising a child. In all honesty, Granny didn't *choose* me, Granny chose to *save* me.

As a result of my mother's discovery, a lot of calls were made, and discussions were had that I was not privy to. All I know is that when I got back to church, James was gone. His mother had sent him away. I was devastated, and I was still learning, but this experience reinforced my belief about love. I understood even more now that love was to be kept secret. That love was something dirty and shameful and although it felt good, love was to be kept silent. Love was not to be shared or boasted. I had to keep love to myself if I wanted to hold on to it. It made sense to my young mind. You see, I loved my mother and she was gone. I loved my father and he was gone. Now I loved this boy and he was gone. In each scenario, something I'd said or done caused their exit from my life. This didn't teach me to stop my search for love, it just taught me to keep my search silent.

CHAPTER 5

Granny was raised by her grandmother, who had fifteen kids of her own. She too knew the pain of living without her parents, maybe that's why she readily accepted the responsibility of raising me. I don't know a lot about her story, but I do remember her often saying that her parents ran off and left her. They dropped her with her grandmother and went on to live their lives, never returning for her. When her mother fell ill with rheumatoid arthritis, Granny took her in and cared for her until she died. That's the type of woman she was. A woman who would overlook years of pain and feelings of abandonment to lovingly care for a woman who didn't do the same for her.

Years later, when her father plunged into the beginning stages of senility, she brought him into our home and cared for him as well. I was around ten or eleven at the time (again hard to remember the ages), and Granddaddy (as we all called him) was this new mysterious being. He was very tall, maybe 6'4, slim, and had red-brown skin, bushy gray eyebrows and matching nose hairs that stuck far out of his nose. It was said that he was half Blackfoot Indian, and his facial features, skin tone and thick silky hair seemed to prove it. He smelled of cigarettes and Old Spice and I loved everything about him.

He was a quiet man, often sitting on our front porch smoking his Lucky Strikes and staring off into space. The tips of his fingers were brown and calloused from smoking his unfiltered cigarettes down to barely a nub. He always sat with his legs crossed and his arms laid across his lap, and I thought it was hilarious because he was so tall that his knees pointed to the sky. He had dentures but hated wearing them, so his bottom jaw sat out at an odd angle, and every day I'd say, *'Granddaddy show me your teeth'*, and roll on the ground in laughter when he'd lower his bottom lip and show me the toothless gums inside. He fascinated me, and I could often be found playing at his feet.

My play time doubled as keeping an eye on him because he'd begun to forget who and where he was. I can remember a time that he walked out of our house believing he was headed to work...on the railroad. It was hard redirecting him, and as time passed, he started to become belligerent and violent. One day, Granny was gone and Granddaddy tried to leave. I did my best to keep him in the house, but when I stood in front of the door to stop him from opening it, he knocked me flat on the floor and left anyway. Realizing that we needed help with him, Granny was still against placing him in a nursing home, so she decided to hire someone to come to the house.

This began as a wonderful idea. The man that she hired was a close friend of the family and well trusted. He was also a minister at our church. We'll call him 'Peter'.

It was summer, so I was at home all day with Granddaddy and Peter. Being raised as an only child, I was used to playing alone unless my cousins were around. Peter would come in the morning and stay until Granny got off work in the evening. During his daily visits, he would make sure that we ate, help Granddaddy get to the bathroom, keep him clean and dressed and handle all of his violent outbursts.

Almost every day, Peter would wait until Granddaddy took his nap, then walk to the corner store for snacks. He always brought me something back, usually an oversized freeze pop because they were my favorite. One day, before he gave me my treat, Peter pulled me into the living room. He told me that I could have my treat, but I needed to lie down first. He assured me that he wasn't going to hurt me. I can remember being nervous, but I didn't know how to say no. He was a grown up, one that I knew, so I felt I could trust him. He was a *preacher*. Besides, Granny left him here at the house, so he must be safe. He ran his hand up my leg, and I turned my head away. He tried to talk to me, but I wasn't very responsive. He told me I was pretty, told me I was a good girl. Then he laid on top of me. *Mask on.*

I remember feeling his weight and finding it difficult to breathe. I remember trying to figure out what he was doing, and why it was making him breathe so hard. I remember the friction felt like carpet burn, because we were both fully clothed. He was rock hard and dry humping me so aggressively that I could feel each poke between my legs. I remember trying to figure out that if we both had our clothes on, why was it wet between my legs. More than anything, I remember my old friend shame rising back to the surface, and I instantly knew this was another secret I needed to keep.

From that day, this became the ritual. He would go to the store, dry hump me until he was satisfied, and then give me my freeze pop and tell me to go outside. I became numb. Like every other time, I fell into the routine of making sure that he wasn't upset with me. He must love me if he wanted to be close to me like this. The love felt strange to me, but in my head, it had to be love. No other explanation made sense, but it was confusing. The mask I wore with Peter was different. It was protective, it hid my true feelings. I was afraid of him. I didn't want his love. I didn't like how his love made me feel, and I was afraid to anger him, so I learned how to go inside of myself. I created characters, families, friends, an alternate universe where I could escape the reality of what was happening to me.

One morning at the beginning of our ritual, Peter asked me to take off my clothes.

"You don't have to if you don't want to, but can you? You're so beautiful. I won't hurt you."

I found myself at a crossroad. I definitely did not want to stand before him naked, but I was afraid that he would be mad at me if I didn't comply, and I wasn't sure what he would do. I stood, eyes staring at the floor while he cooed words of encouragement to me. I was old enough to know this was wrong, but young enough to be scared to death. I had been confused about his love anyway, and the love I knew always involved my body, so maybe this was okay. He called me beautiful. *Wasn't that love?* He promised not to hurt me. *Wasn't that love?* Eventually, I did what he asked me to do, and he resumed his normal position on top of me. He did not take his clothes off, but I could hear my heart beating in my ears. I was cold and hot at the same time. I was afraid to move, afraid to breathe, afraid to think. *Mask on.*

That feeling of helplessness, of ugliness, would unfortunately follow me into several situations as I grew older.

That morning, lying underneath a grown man, feeling his manhood pressed up against me, listening to him grunt and breathe, something in me snapped. This was not love. I didn't know what it was, but I was sure love couldn't feel like this. Love wouldn't make me cry, love wouldn't make me stand naked and exposed. Love wouldn't keep poking and hurting me.

I'm not sure how long this had been going on, or how long the offense would've continued. Part of me believes that Peter was gaining the courage to take his clothes off next, and even today I'm afraid to think of those consequences. I can't explain why I never told before that day. Maybe standing before him naked felt like more of a violation to me. Maybe my subconscious was warning me that this was getting out of hand. Maybe I was tired of playing with the invisible friends in my head. Maybe I just wanted to return to the normal little girl that played outside with no thoughts beyond baby dolls and bike riding. Maybe God was saving me from a situation that I couldn't return from.

Whatever the reason, the next day, when it was time for Granny to go to work, I begged her not to leave me. At first, she gave the normal parental response, but I think something in my plea, something in my tears stopped her. She asked me why I was so against staying home that day, and I just blurted it all out. I remember the look of confusion on her face. The look of defeat. Yet again, we were going through this. I remember believing that she must think it was my fault.

Granny never once said she didn't believe me. She asked her questions as usual and made her calls. Granddaddy ended up in a nursing home, I happily spent the rest of that summer with my cousins and I never had to see Peter again.

Except every Tuesday, Friday, Saturday and Sunday at church...

CHAPTER 6

I should stop here and explain that my life was not all bad. There were also good things happening to me, although at the time I may not have fully understood the impact on my life.

My Uncle Charles (the same uncle who came looking for Dwayne when he beat me) met a woman named Madie when I was three. I fell in love with Madie the moment I met her. She often laughs and tells stories of how I made her sit and watch me sing and dance, always needing to be the center of her attention. At the time she didn't have any children, so I was like her first child. Granny didn't exactly have the time or energy to be chasing behind a rambunctious little girl, so Auntie Madie was my escape, my home away from home, my Dear Abby. She took me shopping, to the movies, the library, and on trips. I remember asking God why He didn't make her my mother. I remember crying to her, wishing she could be my mother. I loved my Granny with all my heart, but losing my parents scarred me, and I was still chasing the love that I'd lost with them.

Auntie was a high school English teacher and also head of the drama club. She was an avid reader and introduced me to the joy of books. I developed an insatiable need to read everything I could get my hands on. She would bring me bags and bags of books that I'd devour and then call her for more. I was already journaling regularly, so it was almost second nature for me to start writing. I began to express myself through poetry around the end of seventh grade. It was liberating to be able to hide my feelings in the rhythm of poetry, to no longer keep my secrets welled up inside of me. Watching my story come to life on paper, while being able to purge myself of the pain and the confusion, saved my life. I have no doubt that without this outlet, and with all the pain left to fester and grow inside of me, I would have grown into a very different person.

I must attribute even the writing of this book to my Aunt Madie. After listening to story after story of my pain, it was she who encouraged me to write about it. I could always tell her anything, and I did. She is the only other person I told about Peter when I was a child. I told her all about my mom and my dad. I told her things that I never told Granny. Everything that I told her made it into my notebook one way or the other. I would write a new piece, call and read it to her, and anxiously await her approval. It became a routine for us. Now I understand that she saw me, the real me, without the mask. God allowed her to see into me. She knew that I needed something, someone, just for me. She saw the train wreck that I was on the inside, and although it wasn't her responsibility, she helped me start the long and intense journey to healing.

Although reading and writing became monumental in my life, they were not my first love. Since the age of two years old, I'd been singing in church. Born into a family of singers, musicians and preachers, it was second nature for me to grab the microphone. I loved the attention, the praise, and especially the look of pride on Granny's face whenever I got up to lead a song. I generally sang with my eyes closed to keep from being nervous, but if I did open them, it was to search out her face, to watch for her expression, to read in the lines around her eyes whether I was honoring God the way that she'd taught me.

"Don't showboat," she'd say. *"You're singing for God, so you don't have to put on a show."*

Whenever my grandmother spoke, it was law to me. There wasn't a person alive who could dispute anything that she'd ever told me. So, when she told me not to showboat, I learned that lesson. In spite of the fact that my mother, uncles and cousins could sing circles around me, doing what I assumed was 'showboating', I followed Granny's instruction and just sang my little heart out. I never did learn how to do all the popular riffing and running and other creative singing tricks that everyone around me were doing, but I believe God honored my straight, flat-footed singing style, and Granny praised my efforts. That meant more to me than anything.

If Auntie Madie and writing were my refuge, then music was my escape. I can vividly remember sitting on the floor of my bedroom with my silver boombox, a notebook, a blank cassette tape and the radio tuned to *FM 98 WJLB*. I recorded every Whitney Houston song that came on the air, then I'd start the painful play-stop-rewind-play process that ensured I could write down every lyric. I'd close my door so Granny couldn't hear me singing that 'worldly' music, and belt out every note, word for word, with tears streaming down my face. Songs like *Where Do Broken Hearts Go* and *Didn't We Almost Have It All* rendered me breathless in ways that were completely familiar and totally confusing for me. I didn't understand the lyrics from an adult relationship perspective, but I understood the *feelings* they represented all too well. Whitney became my shero, both for her vocal acrobatics and her ability to instantly melt my mask, exposing my insides like a surgeon on an operating table.

By the time I got to Cass Technical High School I had put the two together and was writing my own songs. I even had a short-lived rap career and a singing group. I had found a way to wade through the mud of my emotions. I still needed my mask from time to time, but I now had a way to matriculate through the real world, unaccompanied by some of the weight I had been dragging around for years.

I filled page upon page with my pain, my disappointments and my need for love. It was like releasing the steam from a radiator.

CHAPTER 7

Up to this point, I'd really only known my mother's side of the family. Besides Nanny, who Granny would take me to see on holidays for about thirty minutes, I never saw anyone from my dad's side. I remembered my Uncle Tony who I adored and my dad's mom, who I wasn't very close to, but that was about it. In contrast, I was very close to all of my other aunts, uncles and cousins. I was raised with my cousins, but we were more like siblings. My uncles were my daddies, looking after me for Granny, spoiling me, and trying to make sure I didn't turn out like my mother. And of course, there was Aunt Madie. I loved my family, and always wanted to be around them, but I also started to question my identity.

Why did I like red licorice when everyone else loved black? Why did I always feel like something was missing when so many people seemed to love me? Why was my taste in music so different? And most confusing, why was I thinking about my father again??

I can still remember the afternoon that I built up enough nerve to tell my Granny that I wanted to see my dad. I could see her measure her breathing, working hard to control her facial reaction. She asked me why. I told her because I wanted to know the other side of my family. I wanted to know my two younger brothers. I had questions about myself that didn't fit with this side of my DNA. She asked me was I sure. I told her yes. She took a deep breath, said okay, and that she'd make the call.

Word spread through my family fast, and I could tell everyone thought I'd lost my mind. I remember all the whispered conversations. I remember speaking to Auntie Madie about it. One of the amazing things about my aunt is she never pretends like she agrees if she doesn't, but she genuinely tries to understand your position. I knew my decision wouldn't be a popular one, but I commend my family for sticking by me, and allowing me to experience my journey the way *I* needed to. A few days later, Granny handed me the phone, and my dad was on the other end.

My heart felt swollen and about to burst. There were tears in my eyes, and I was nervous. Actually, I was scared, but I didn't really know why. Our conversation was brief and ended with him setting a day and time to come and visit. There was a mixture of dread and excitement building inside me, and I didn't know on which side of the line I should fall. Imagine a fourteen-year-old girl who had been physically and sexually abused multiple times. Imagine her spending so many of her days longing for her parents, the people who were supposed to love and protect her. Imagine her trying to understand why they didn't, why she wasn't important enough, why there was so much pain in her belly. Then imagine her trying to tear that part of her longing out, and not being able to. Already rejected by a drug addicted mother, I guess something in me just needed to see if any of it was salvageable.

The day he came to the house, he was in a black older model Mercedes Benz, and he parked across the street. I watched him from the door of the top porch, and I had no clue what to do, or how to react. Half of me wanted to run and jump in his arms. The other half wanted to scream at him and punch him and ask him why.

Why didn't you love me enough to just be my daddy?

Why did you let all this stuff happen to me?

Why couldn't you give me my picket fence?

As it turns out, I did neither. He came in the house and we sat at the dining room table. Ironically, my mother was also there, and Granny of course. He smelled of some popular cologne that filled my nostrils with memories of my childhood. His face and hair were pristine. His outfit carefully selected and matching from head to toe. The sun was shining brightly, and I remember thinking the whole scene was phony. It couldn't really be happening. He hugged my grandmother. She was cordial but cool. He hugged my mother. She fawned over him. He didn't try to hug me at first, letting me take the lead. We sat and talked a bit. He asked me about school, told me about my brothers, made me laugh. I sat there trying to remember why I hated him. Trying to understand why we'd been apart so long. Trying to make all the pieces fit.

I decided in that moment that I wanted to know him. He owed me that much. He owed me the other side of my family. He owed me time. He owed me whatever the hell I wanted, because he was the daddy not me. He was the one who messed it all up, not me.

I can imagine what you're thinking, and I understand. How on earth could I ever want to be in the presence of this man? How could I ever want any type of relationship with him? What the hell was wrong with me? I can't answer those questions for you, at least not with the answers you may be seeking. All I can tell you is what my thought process was, and how I justified it in my head. I was raised in a family that taught you to forgive seventy times seven. I was raised in church, where principles and guidelines were forced down your throat. I took it all seriously. I asked myself over and over why it would be wrong to forgive everyone else and not him. I asked myself was there something wrong with me, that I would want to see him. I asked myself what was I trying to accomplish. Unlike my mom, who still seemed to only care about herself, who didn't even love me enough to leave drugs completely alone, he was here, knowing how uncomfortable it would be, knowing he was being judged every second. That meant something, right?

I can't honestly tell you the answers I came up with at the time. What I can say in hindsight is that there is a vein of love that flows through me that I've never been able to suppress. Although I understood what happened to me was molestation, I desperately wanted to be a daddy's girl. I wanted to have 'normal' parents and experiences and I was willing to make the sacrifices needed to have them. Just like that, I wiped the slate clean. Or at least I tried to. I decided to start over, to give him another chance to prove he deserved me. My mom had been given multiple chances, why not my dad? I decided to move forward the only way I knew how, with my heart open and expectations high.

I know the child psychologists are going to have a field day with this, and that's ok. They didn't live my life, or think my thoughts, or feel my feelings. I know that I will be bashed in the public eye for choosing to have a relationship with what the world calls a pedophile. I know that my decision won't be respected by many, but the decision I made that day changed the trajectory of my life, my dad's life and the lives of everyone closely involved with me.

The one thing my dad couldn't hide was his visible relief. His astonishment that he was sitting across from me and I wasn't shunning him. It was that day that I saw in him something broken, and I wanted to know what it was. Keep in mind, I didn't know any of his familial history at this time. However, I saw into him that day, and a need to understand him was birthed in me.

INTERLUDE: DEANDRE

L et me pause here.

Based on societal views, everything about the relationship that I now have with my father is wrong. I shouldn't see him, speak to him, spend time with him, and I definitely shouldn't allow him around my children.

I want to address this, because I understand the thought process, and I know there are and will be tons of questions.

I'm going to start by saying that I will never try to appease everyone on this, because that would be impossible. There will always be those that think I'm nuts, and that's okay. My experience and how I chose to handle it is my own, and I understand that it wouldn't have worked for everyone. I will however, do my best to explain how it worked for me, and why I was able to move past what happened to me, and allow my father a place in my life, a place that I control, a place with boundaries that he no longer tries to push.

As I stated in Chapter 7, the largest press for reuniting with my dad was my search for identity. There were so many things about me that didn't add up to the maternal side of my family, and I didn't understand why. Because I was never brutalized like some sexual molestation victims, I never had a fear of my father. I didn't jump when he came in the room, I didn't know to be disgusted by him, the typical feelings generally discussed never developed in me. Once it was discovered and Granny made me understand what had happened to me, I was still very confused. You have to understand who my Granny was. She was an evangelist, very spiritual, and very closed-mouthed about most things. The words that I've previously shared are pretty much all that she gave me (dirty, filthy, dog). She told me that what he did was wrong, but never in detail, never why.

As I grew older, I was violated over and over, never having gotten a true understanding in the beginning. Perhaps had this never happened, or had someone truly helped me to understand, I wouldn't have been taken advantage of so many times. For me, the main question was why. Why would he do this to me if it was wrong? Why didn't I know it was wrong? Why couldn't a father be close to a daughter? I'd seen my mother in compromising positions tons of times with her boyfriends, that was love to me. Daddy loved me, right? I was so young, and had seen so much, I was totally confused. If it was so wrong, why did it keep happening to me? Back then, I think the elders believed that children were too young to understand things of this nature, so it was never really discussed.

I grew up and figured out why it was wrong for him to do, but then I was obsessed with why he would do it. I blamed myself. I blamed him. I tried to figure it out. On top of all of this, my body was going through changes that I had no way of understanding, and that I wouldn't dare tell anyone about. Everything about my life was secret, made up. I wore the mask even at seven years old.

When I decided to allow my dad back into my life, it wasn't all roses and ice cream. I was afraid of him, but I hid it. He was this entity that I remembered but didn't know. He was and still is very affectionate, always looking for a hug or a kiss. I didn't know how to feel about that. I'd been conditioned, however, to please, so when he wanted a hug, I gave him one. Outwardly, I'm sure I seemed fine, inwardly, I cringed in the beginning. I didn't know how to react. I didn't know how to feel, and I didn't know how to say any of this to anyone.

My dad is very charismatic. He's charming, handsome, very personable. Everywhere he goes, people love him, especially the women. He's very open, brutally honest, and terribly descriptive. As a teenager, I had no idea how to handle this, so I fell into my typical habit of making sure I didn't piss him off. It's how I handled everything in those days. I was still walking the street that love had paved for me, and I didn't know anything else to do. I was way too involved in his relationships, he was way too involved in mine, and I didn't have enough guts to stand up for myself. Somewhere inside of me, that little girl was screaming that if we pissed him off, he'd leave.

There was also the fact that I was a typical teenager, being raised by an older woman who could care less about the trends of the day. For the first time in my life, thanks to my dad, I had name brand clothes and shoes. I was getting my hair done in a real salon. I was walking around in popular jewelry and perfume. I no longer looked like I belonged in one of Granny's mail order catalogs, nor was I wearing my best friend's clothes just so I could fit in at school. I had money in my pocket and somebody to call when I wanted something. That felt good. To a girl who dressed most of her life out of the hand me down boxes, that felt wonderful.

The good outweighed the bad for me. I was able to ignore the little feelings in my gut when he wanted a hug until eventually they weren't there. When I began to meet the other side of my family, it was even better. There was Aunt Mikoe, only ten years older than me (my dad's sister), that became my pride and joy. She was young and beautiful and stylish, with a huge house, a sports car, a husband and a diamond ring so big you couldn't see her hand around it. She was teaching me etiquette, buying me clothes, and taking me out to eat. She was throwing me parties and inviting my friends over. She was who I wanted to be. She had my life, and I studied everything about her. I wanted to be her. I hated her just as much as I loved her. Why did she get the perfect life while I got left with the crap?

There were grandparents that always had parties and let me invite my friends. We could listen to 'worldly' music all night and dance, and if you were quick, you could sneak a little nip of whatever was in their cups. There were cut throat card games and 'bones' thrown on tables. There were pots that you shouldn't eat out of because granddaddy might've killed a possum that day. There were huge Christmas trees and sleepovers just for me. There was laughter and fun and foolishness and I loved every bit of it. It's not that I didn't have fun and family on Granny's side, I did, and I loved that too, but this was different. It felt forbidden somehow. It felt like a Neverland reserved just for me, and I didn't want to give it up. The key to this world was my dad. It never once dawned on me that I could have all of them without him, and

I never tried.

Like every other time in my life, I pushed through whatever feelings I may have had, and just lived in the moment. There were some bumps along the way, times when I had to confide in Aunt Mikoe that I was uncomfortable, that I was unsure. We had some hard conversations that to this day I've never shared with anyone else, but I didn't get the strength to stand up for myself until I became a mother. Every part of me changed when I looked that baby in the face for the first time, and this was no different.

My daughter was an infant and we had our own place when I finally confronted my dad about our past. All the years of wanting to know why, of needing to hear him say it, of needing him to acknowledge what he did caught up with me. As a parent, I couldn't imagine ever hurting my child, violating or betraying her, confusing her in the ways that he had done to me. Becoming a mother gave me a confidence that I'd never had. All the fear that I'd stored seemed to seep out of me like it was never there. I went to his house and faced him and asked him why. I asked how he could ever do what he did to me.

I won't lie and tell you that he had a 'good' answer. He didn't. How could you have a good answer to that question? I do, however, believe that he answered me honestly. Here's the thing, my dad took full responsibility for his actions. He didn't blame his life or his circumstances. He didn't blame my mother or me. He didn't blame his upbringing or his environment. He blamed himself. He never told me how he grew up, the stories that would've made sense to me, the things he saw that would've been burned in his mind. Unlike my mother, never once did he try to blame anyone else for how he violated me. He answered all my questions. He cried. He apologized. He thanked me for allowing him into my life. He thanked me for not keeping my daughter away from him. He acknowledged that most people in my situation would never have come back. He asked for my forgiveness.

For me, that was enough. I needed at least one of my parents to acknowledge that they'd done me wrong. I needed to hear that I wasn't crazy, that I'd been hurt, that these things never should've been done to me. I needed one of them to love me enough to try and make it right. I'd been searching for those words for almost twenty years, but by the time I'd gotten them, I'd already made too many bad decisions. The trajectory of my life was set on a course that I didn't yet see as dangerous. Still, the process started that day. I began to mend that day. It began to unravel that day.

It has been a long process since that day almost fifteen years ago setting up boundaries in my life for my father. It's hard for me to set up boundaries for men in my life period because of him, but I have come a long way. There are times when I won't talk to him at all. I don't call. I don't go by. I don't answer calls. It's unspoken, but he gets the point, and he doesn't press it. In some ways, I'm still not as strong as I'd like to be. I still don't say the words, I just disappear. My daughter used to ask often if she could spend the night at his house, the answer was always no. My children adore my dad, and I will never do anything to harm their relationship, but it doesn't change the fact that sometimes the hair on the back of my neck still stands up. Sometimes it's still hard to give him a hug. I watch how he hugs them, how close they sit next to him on the couch watching a movie. These are all things that I cannot help and will not apologize for.

The point is, I've learned what I will and will not accept from him. When it becomes too much, I shut it down. That is how it works for me. That may seem crazy to all of you, but you didn't live my life. I'm grateful that I was able to ask him the hard questions. That I didn't drive myself to drugs or alcohol searching for answers I never would've been able to give myself. I pray every day for the people that have yet to gain that freedom, or that died searching for it. I'm grateful that although certain parts of our relationship will never be salvaged, my dad was able to redeem himself through my children and show our family that he is not a monster. I'm grateful that I can see him in a different light. That I was there the day he fell on his face and begged God to forgive him. I'm grateful that God placed a heart in me that allows me to see past what has been done to me, and to keep on forgiving, keep on loving, keep on trying, even when others don't deserve it. I'm grateful that although I know I've birthed some generational curses into my children, I've also stood strong enough to identify and break some of them.

My dad is not perfect, but neither are any of us. He didn't lie. He didn't make excuses, which I will always commend him for. That took guts most men in his position never display. God loves him just as much as He loves me. I don't excuse what he did to me, but I don't stand in the way of God's redeeming power in his life either.

CHAPTER 8

School was a different experience for me. I had never been the pretty girl, or the popular girl, or even the girl with the cute clothes. Granny had way more on her mind than making sure I was fashionable and fit in with the other kids. As matter of fact, I don't even think she thought about it. On Sundays, I was the best dressed little girl in the building, but during the week, it was enough for her if I was neat, clean and covered. For me, however, this was the most important time of my life. My self-esteem took a hit. I believed I was ugly because most of the boys told me I was. I latched on to any friend I could, all while secretly wishing the 'cool kids' would like me. That never happened.

By the time I made it to high school, I was used to being an outsider, and no longer cared. I loved the friends I had and didn't worry about the ones I didn't (well, most of the time anyway). The first day of ninth grade, I made a complete fool of myself by sitting in the only desk that didn't have a chair attached and falling on my butt in front of the entire class. Ears burning with shame and staring at the floor willing it to open up and swallow me, a hand reached down to help me up. That hand was attached to the girl who would become my forever best friend, Chelsea (Jones) Anderson. She took me in like a stray and taught me how to style my hair, how to dress cute on a budget and how to stop worrying about what I didn't have or what I couldn't do. Ironically, I had a friend named Erna Mitchell in middle school who transferred to another middle school where she and Chelsea became friends and the three of us all ended up in Cass together.

Having secured my friend base, I walked with a different level of confidence, and the worries of middle school fell off my shoulders. This cleared me up to continue my secret quest for love. On the outside, I looked like any other boy-crazy teenage girl. I sang love songs to an imaginary boy. I stayed in the mirror trying to be cute for a nonexistent boyfriend if I was single, or the catch-of-the-week if I wasn't. I imagined myself married with babies and having a house with a white picket fence. In my head, I created for myself the life I'd always wished I had.

My last summer before high school, I met a boy named Jay. Even though he was one year younger than me, everything about him appealed to me. His dark complexion. His dark brown eyes. His skinny legs. His huge grin. The way he carried himself like a grown man, even though he was only thirteen years old. His eyes told a story that I wanted to read. And when he looked at me, he made me melt. He told me I was the prettiest girl in the world. He made me blush, giggle and laugh all at the same time. He was the first person to look beyond my second-hand clothes, my basement salon hairdo, and my dark skin and love every bit of me. At fourteen years old, I fell hard, and he became my first real boyfriend.

Because I entered high school with a boyfriend, I didn't feel the same pressure that most girls did to get attention from the boys. I did, however, try to spend every unoccupied moment with Jay. It wasn't long before I was skipping school to spend the day with him. One of my fondest memories is of settling into my English class one morning but having this overwhelming feeling to look out of the window. I got up and looked out to see Jay and his brother Frankie (who had recently started dating one of my friends) standing in the parking lot directly across the street. I showed my friend and we slid past security and into their arms. We spent the day downtown at Hart Plaza, at Lafayette Coney Island, and ducking the truancy cops. The guys doted on us and made us feel safe. They were over protective and almost possessive, but we loved every minute of it.

There was something different about Jay and me. We seemed to need and understand love in a way most teens our age couldn't. I told him my life story, all of it. He didn't judge. He told me his life story, all if it. I didn't judge. Jay was what society would call a 'thug'. He fought often, had a chip on his shoulder, and was deeply protective over those he loved. He was brilliant but didn't really care much about school. He took the test for Cass because I was there, and of course, he passed and was accepted. But the atmosphere at Cass was too academic for him. He was used to leaving when he wanted, skipping classes, fighting and chasing girls. None of which he could do (successfully) at Cass. He was soon kicked out.

The beauty in our relationship didn't come from school or even the neighborhood. Very early on, Jay and I realized that our connection was unusual. He could literally think a color, word or phrase and I would guess it, and vice versa. (We won a lot of bets doing this, lol). As hard as he was with the outside world, he was just as soft with me. The only other person I ever saw him display that same type of feeling with was his mother. In the mornings, whether he went to school or not, he would walk all the way up to Jefferson to get the bus with me and ride to school. He would listen to me vent about my parents or whatever was ailing me at the time, and he would hold me, wipe my tears, tell me he loved me. And I believed him. In fact, I *knew* it was true. I could feel his heart. I could see his love in his eyes. All of the love that I was missing from my parents, I found in Jay. He gave me all the attention I needed. He never let anything or anyone keep us apart.

Meanwhile, of course Granny hated him. She saw him as a little hood boy with bad intentions and she was having none of that. What she didn't count on, though, was the intensity of our love. We just got smarter and sneakier. Let's be clear: Jay and I were not having, nor did we have sex. That was one thing I had no interest in back then. I loved to kiss and hug and rub and cuddle, but that was as far as it went for me. Based on the nature of our relationship, I think that Jay always felt we would just naturally evolve into having sex. I mean I went home with MANY a non-disappearing hickey in my day. MANY! Sex was not what I wanted though. I wanted what I had, to feel safe and loved and adored. To feel pretty. To know that someone would fight for me. I had all of that without sex, so what was the point? By the beginning of tenth grade, we had broken up.

Our stories differ on this, but from my perspective, he was ready to get down and I wasn't. Plenty of girls were throwing it at him, and eventually, he gave in. He cheated on me, I somehow found out, and my heart was yet again broken.

Once more, something I did, or rather *didn't* do, led to me losing the love of my life. Love was still teaching me. It was still eluding me. However, something unique and different happened to me as it pertained to Jay. He opened a part of my heart that I never knew existed. In the deepest corners of my heart and brain I knew that our love was special. That it was more than puppy love. I knew that he had imprinted on me and would always be a part of me. He knew it too. From then until now, he still comes if I call. I still get an overwhelming feeling when he's going through and just needs to hear my voice. My children adore him. My grandmother grew to love him, and up until her death called him *her* 'boyfriend'. He is indeed connected to my soul. As adults, we tried to rekindle the relationship from long ago, but it wasn't to be. I'm not sure he at first understood when I told him that we could never be together that way, as husband and wife. That our love was meant for something different. That God gave us what we needed at that time. That marriage isn't our path. I will always be grateful for the part he played in my life, and I love him enough to let him go.

I stopped to give you the background on Jay because I've spent the rest of my life looking for the intensity of that love. I've gone from relationship to relationship waiting on someone to love me so much that they'd give their life for me. So much that they'd fight a giant for me. So much that they'd never leave...like everyone else.

CHAPTER 9

I would love to be able to tell you that after all of the sexual abuse I'd already endured, life moved on and I was never violated again; but I can't tell you that.

The year I turned eighteen, my dad bought us tickets to the Teena Marie concert. His birthday was seven days before mine, and that night he was having a huge party. The plan was for us to go to the concert with a couple of his friends, and then back to the hotel, where I had a room of my own. I wasn't allowed to go up to the room where the party was taking place, but I didn't care, because it was all about the concert to me. I absolutely loved Teena Marie and had been anticipating her show for weeks.

My dad has always been very particular about his appearance, and whenever he goes anywhere, he meticulously plans his outfit weeks in advance. That night was no different. He was laid from his Dobb to his gators and our group walked into the *Fox* with all eyes on us. I wore a long, form-fitting black and white block dress that laid perfectly against every curve I had, and in 1995, my stomach was flat, and my curves were in all the right places. During this time, my childhood asthma had returned, and I had just began suffering from migraines, so it had been a while since I could go out and have any fun. I was looking forward to screaming my head off and trying to match Teena note for note on all my favorite songs. It turned out to be one of the best nights I'd had in a long time.

After the concert, although I was still excited and happy, I was exhausted and physically weak. I went to my room and immediately got ready for bed. I was still taking multiple medications to manage the asthma and migraines, some of which made me sleep heavily, so I knew my night was over. My dad and one of his friends left some of their bags in the room with me, told me where to find them in case of an emergency, and that they'd see me in the morning.

Sometime in the middle of the night, I heard a noise. I remember trying to sit up, but being so groggy, that I couldn't really lift my head like I wanted. I smelled the strong stench of alcohol, but I wasn't alarmed at first. Only the people that came with me had a key to the room. I felt the bed give, and for some reason, my stomach dropped. Some inner warning bell went off in my head. It was dark in the room, but when he spoke, I recognized the voice of my dad's friend. He was saying something that I couldn't understand, and I asked him to repeat it. I asked him where my dad was.

He got on top of me.

This man was muscular, with the upper torso of a bodybuilder. I was about 140 lbs and under the influence of medication. I asked him to get off of me. I tried to roll to the right, and he grabbed my arms. I knew that he was talking to me, but I couldn't understand what he was saying. It was almost like he was rambling to himself but wanting me to respond. I realized that he was completely inebriated, and that's when the real fear rolled in. I asked him again to get off me. What I didn't know was that he had taken off his clothes before he walked to the bed. I couldn't breathe. The liquor on his breath was stifling to me. His body was hot and hard and pressing.

He yanked up my nightgown.

"Please don't do this."

My one plea.

The tears streamed from my eyes. I tried to get out of his grip. I tried to will myself off the bed. He told me not to 'fucking move'. I thought about how heavy he was, and how easy it would be for him to hurt me. I thought about the other times, how being pressed underneath him reminded me of Peter. I thought about every time I've been violated, every time something was taken from me.

I stopped fighting. *Mask on.*

I turned my head away from his face, with tears still streaming from my eyes, and forced my mind to leave my body.

No, I didn't scream. No, I didn't cry out for help.

I just learned a new lesson. I learned to suffer in silence. To hold my breath and wait until the pain was over.

When he was done, he got up and went back where he came from.

Numb. Angry. Sad. Stupid.

These were my feelings.

What was it about me that kept inviting people to violate me? To disrespect me in the worst way?

What was I doing wrong?

What was wrong with me??

I didn't tell my dad, or anyone, right away. Can you imagine the irony of telling my dad this story? I went back home and tried to make myself forget it ever happened. I was doing a good job too, until I started to itch and burn. Worse than telling my dad was telling my grandmother, but I had no choice. I knew I needed to go to the doctor.

The visit at the doctor's office was brutal. The embarrassment of telling them why I was there. Answering all the questions. Seeing the look on my grandmother's face. Feeling the disappointment in myself for failing her once again. Before the rape, I had only had sex with one other person in my life, and yet here I sat, dirty. We listened as the doctor rattled off my test results:

Chlamydia.

Gonorrhea.

Trichomonas.

Dirty.

Dog.

I spent most of my teenage years avoiding sex so that my grandmother wouldn't think I was a dirty dog. I'd waited until the last half of my senior year of high school, and still sometimes felt bad that I'd ever given in at all. Despite my efforts, I was once again looking at the disgust in my grandmother's face. I now know that her disgust was never directed towards me, but I didn't understand that then. Every new situation revived the little girl that lived inside me. She was battered, abused and rejected. She believed it was all her fault. She believed she'd let everyone down. She was still searching.

After we left the doctor, Granny insisted that I call my dad. Another extremely painful and awkward conversation to add to the list of many. It was during this conversation that I learned about the pregnant wife of the man who raped me. My dad has this controlled type of anger. In fact, unless you know him personally, it's almost impossible to guess his feelings. He didn't blow up. He didn't scream or cuss. He asked minimal questions, but after a few days that man disappeared. To this day, I've never asked. I've never cared. But the one thing I do know is he never came around again.

I couldn't stop thinking about the unborn baby, who was innocent, who didn't deserve this. I even thought about the wife, and how she had no clue her husband was an animal. The idea of her or the baby getting sick because I wasn't woman enough to warn her played over and over in my head. In the end, my heart won, and I figured out how to contact her. I didn't identify myself. I didn't even tell her that it was rape. I just told her that I'd had sex with her husband and the diseases I'd contracted as a result. She cussed me out, called me a bunch of names and hung up on me.

I moved on.

PART TWO: ILEENE

My Senses

I have eyes, which means I can see.
I can see the wonders of the world,
I can see the detail of the rose,
I can see the beauty of the butterfly,
And I can see the sadness in my eyes.
I have a nose, which means I can smell.
I can smell the sweet nectar of a flower,
I can smell the pollution surrounding my city,
I can smell the smoke of an enraging fire,
And I can smell the hatred pouring from my body.
I have a mouth, which means I can taste.
I can taste the coolness of water on a hot day,
I can taste the sweetness of caramel
as it rolls down my throat,
I can taste the fire of a red hot pepper,
And I can taste the salt of my tears.
I have ears, which means I can hear.
I can hear the sound of soft, soothing jazz,
I can hear the ripple of the waves,
I can hear the cry of an upset child,
And I can hear the bitterness protruding from my voice.
I have hands, which means I can feel.
I can feel the softness of a newborn baby,
I can feel the rough edge of the most beautiful rock,
I can feel the smoothness of a velvet petal,
And I can feel the pain engulfing my heart.
~Shaquenia Witherspoon - 10th Grade~

CHAPTER 10

Ileene, my mother, was the youngest of Granny's five children, and also the only girl. Three of my uncles were from Granny's first husband, Rev. A. B. Searcy Jr, and my mother and one more uncle were from my grandfather, Rev. Joseph Lee Irving.

I don't know a lot about Rev. Irving, but here's what I do know:

He was about twenty-six years older than my grandmother. He was a Pastor. He was heralded as one of the best preachers and singers on the eastside of Detroit. He was in a popular quartet called the Flying Clouds of Detroit. And in Granny's words, he was an alcoholic and a whoremonger.

Granny once shared with me the story about a meeting where they were summoned to the church my grandfather was pastoring and the board asked him to step down. There was evidence that he had slept with multiple women in the congregation, including some of the deacons' wives. The most poignant part of this story for me is how Granny described feeling so small, praying profusely for God to allow the floor to open up and swallow her whole. My grandmother, the First Lady of the church, made to look and feel like a fool.

She did not leave him. In fact, they went on to found a church of their own of which she remained a member until the day she died. She told me that she stopped sleeping in the bed with him, stopped having sex with him, and just kept living her life. She had five children to worry about and he was a good provider. She did what she'd been conditioned to do...move on.

I bring up this small piece of history to give a bit of a background on my mother. Just like with my dad, I feel that it's important to know where she came from to understand where she ended up. My grandfather, obviously, had some addictive behaviors. Alcohol, maybe even sex, and whatever chemical imbalance there was inside of him passed down to his children. My grandfather died when my mother was about twelve years old. From my understanding, they were extremely close, and she was never the same after his death. Granny said this is when she started hanging with the wrong crowd, smoking, drinking and breaking the rules. Three years later, she was pregnant with me.

My parents met in high school (both also attended Cass Technical High School) and fell in love. My dad was two years her senior and said that he initially looked at her as a little sister, but Ileene was having none of that. My dad was tall, dark and handsome, and with his background, I'm sure he appealed to the little girl parts of her that missed her father and wanted to be loved and protected (a similarity that we shared as young women choosing men).

As the story goes, my dad told my mother he wanted a baby, and she willingly obliged. They went to my dad's house one day (where he lived with Nanny), and she allowed them to go in the basement and conceive me. Based on the stories, I have to believe that finding out she was pregnant was bittersweet for my mother. Telling my dad had to make her the happiest she'd been in a while. He'd wanted a baby, and she was able to give him one. Surely their love was set in stone now that they'd become parents.

However, telling my grandmother garnered an entire different response. If I'm to believe the story the way Ileene told it, Granny cornered her in the bathroom, lifted her by her neck and told her how stupid she was. (I'm apt to believe this, because with the exception of the neck part, Granny spent thirty minutes telling me how stupid I was when I disclosed I was pregnant at twenty-three). This had to be traumatizing for my mother, and I would never make light of that. I believe that my mother was searching for someone to love her, and for someone that she could pour all her love into. She found part of that in my dad, and after losing her own father, wanted to do whatever she could to hold on to it. Being the only girl in a house full of boys, plus having a mother with sometimes impossibly high expectations would be hard for anyone. I'm not sure she ever thought about what being a teen mom would mean, or the ramifications of her decision. She just wanted a family to call her own.

In stark contrast, my grandmother was a first lady. She was an evangelist. She was a pillar in the community. She was called on to speak all over the country. She held several titles in the church, the district and elsewhere. Having a fifteen-year-old pregnant daughter didn't fit into the mold of her life. Her children were scholars, athletes, active in the church. They sang in the choir, they were junior deacons, and active in the youth department. They were not teenage parents.

Being as close to my grandmother as I was throughout my life, I feel comfortable enough to say that she also held a measure of guilt over herself. What had she done wrong that her only daughter, her baby girl, could go so horribly awry? What did her baby need that she hadn't provided? How had she failed her?

My grandmother was not one to discuss her feelings. She would display her reactions, but never the thoughts or feelings that got her there. Once she assessed a situation, she decided what her stance would be and forged ahead against all odds. This probably kept her sane many times over the years of her life. Ileene was emotional though. She has always needed tangible and often publicized acts of expression to feel loved. She needed Granny to hold her and say it was ok. She needed Granny to tell her that no matter what, she was proud of her. She needed Granny to not only say 'I love you', but to prove it by going against everything she believed to support her. She needed Granny to be the fairytale, the made-up dream of a mother that was in her head, not understanding that Granny never had a mother either. She was abandoned by her mother and father. She never had the fairytale.

So, the story goes that my father went into the Air Force. He knew he had a family to take care of, and the military was his best choice, with housing and other perks available. He came home on leave with a ring and asked my grandmother if he could marry Ileene. In no uncertain terms, she refused to give permission for her sixteen-year-old child (who was also a mother now) to become his wife.

I can imagine the fury Ileene felt. The disappointment. The pain. I can almost see her watching her dreams swirl down the drain. Although I didn't become a mother until I was twenty-three, I was helplessly in love with my ex-husband. No matter what anyone said to me, I wanted to be with him, and the thought of losing him took my breath away. My mother loved my dad like this. In fact, she still does to this day. I've heard her say many times that Granny ruined her life. That she shouldn't have interfered with her family. That everything would have been different had Granny just stayed out of it. Like every other teenaged girl, she thought she had it all figured out. She'd found a man to love, gave him the baby he wanted, and now she was ready to complete the dream.

Whether or not I want to admit it, I see a lot of myself in my mother's story. The longing for the fairytale. The quest for love and acceptance. The clinging to a man, more out of need than anything else. The need for protection, the need for love, the need to be needed. She birthed these needs into me, and I in turn birthed them into my children.

Ileene decided to follow my dad into the service. By the time she got there, however, he had married another woman and moved on with his life. This pain had to join forces with the other, and I believe it created a point of no return for my mother.

CHAPTER 11

By the time I started high school, Ileene had been in and out of rehab several times. The year I decided to see my dad again, she was on one of her clean streaks, and was staying at the house with me and Granny. This was stressful for everyone in the house.

One part of me was happy to have my mother there. I loved her. I missed her. I wanted her to be my mother. The other part of me was angry, hurt and resentful because I still didn't understand our relationship. I didn't understand why so many things took precedence over me in her life. I didn't understand why it was Granny who rescued me and not her.

My mother viewed this time as her chance to reinsert herself as an authority figure in my life. She was jealous of the relationship that Granny and I had, and she was ready for me to see her as my mother. To this day, that has been a losing battle for her. Although Ileene was in the house with us, when I wanted something or needed something, I asked Granny. If Ileene told me to do something, I asked Granny if I had to. I think I looked for reasons to get her in trouble, to 'tell on her'. It was more like we were sisters, and I was the favorite.

I believe Granny was really trying to pull us together. She wanted my mother to have a real chance. She wanted to believe that she would stay clean each time. She needed to believe that she could fix this. Maybe on some levels she felt responsible.

It was too late though. I resented my mother, my mother resented Granny and Granny was caught in the middle. No matter what happened, Granny took my side, and when I realized this, I used it to my advantage. Today I understand that I was just acting out my feelings, trying to make her suffer for the suffering I'd endured. I was trying to make her see me and what she had done to me.

Granny never really left us alone, but once she had to go out of town for the National Baptist Convention. Ileene had been there long enough that she decided to trust her to keep me while she was away. I was around sixteen-years-old and was working a co-op job through my school. My mother had apparently fallen off the wagon, and when I got home from school one day, she started asking me for money. Based on my mother's history, no one in the family would ever really give her large sums of money, and I surely wasn't going to give her anything. By this time, I was a smart-mouthed teenager, with my own job, my own friends, and my own mind. I spent my spare time being mean to her, or at least coming up with ways to let her know that she would NEVER be my mother, and I know that had to hurt her tremendously.

"Shaquenia, give me $20," she asked.

"I don't have any money," I replied.

"Yes you do. It's Friday, you got paid today. Just give me $30, I'll pay you back."

"Funny how quickly it jumped from $20 to $30. I don't have any money," I say again, rolling my eyes and not even looking up in her direction.

That's probably what helped to set her off. The fact that I didn't even respect her enough to look her in the face. She walked into my room and started grabbing my backpack and my purse. I jumped up off my bed and snatched my bag.

"Don't touch my stuff and get out my room!" I yelled.

Ileene was furious by now, and let go of the bag, but grabbed for me. In reality, it all happened very fast. The slap on the side of my head. The bag being thrown into my stomach. Her knocking me into the window. Her grabbing my red tank top to snatch me closer and hit me some more. Me holding up my arms in defense to block as many blows as I could. Her pulling my hair while calling me bitches and yelling other obscenities. What I remember most though, is feeling like I was watching from outside of myself. I remember reminding myself that Granny wouldn't want me to hit her back. That she was still my mother, and it was disrespectful to raise my hand to her. I remember trying to evade her blows and get away, but she had me cornered in my room.

And then she said it.

"I wish I woulda flushed you down the toilet when I had the chance!"

The words I'll never forget. The words that deflated me. The words that screamed my worth to her, or lack thereof. The words that told me she didn't really love me, didn't want me.

Ironically, my dad rescued me this time. I ran downstairs barefoot, with my shirt torn and bloody. The tenant below us let me use the phone, and my dad showed up shortly thereafter and took me to his house with his new wife. I didn't go back home until Granny returned from her trip.

Granny was furious when she found out what happened. Always my hero, I remember swelling with pride when she told Ileene to never lay another hand on me, that she'd 'break her neck', that she 'oughta be ashamed'; I swelled not because of the threats, but because Granny stood up for me, something that up until that point, only she had done. All I'd ever wanted was to belong to the people that claimed to love me, I wanted them to fight for me, to show the world that I mattered more than anything or anyone else. The only person that showed me that kind of love and devotion was Granny, and I would spend the rest of my life trying to give it back to her.

Granny never gave up hope that Ileene would turn her life around. She never stopped impressing upon me the need to love and respect my mother, no matter what she did or how it made me feel. But no matter what we went through or how I acted out, Granny always chose me.

CHAPTER 12

As an adult, I can now see that Ileene and I were both longing for the same thing.

She wanted me to love her more than anyone else. She needed to mean the world to me, because I meant the world to her. She conceived me in the greatest love of her life, and she poured all of that love into me the best way she knew how.

What she saw was her mother receiving the love that was hers, getting the respect she felt she deserved. What she saw in my eyes should belong to her, except I wasn't looking for her. I didn't want her. I didn't love her.

On the other side, I wanted her to love me more than anyone else. I needed to be more important than the men, the drugs...my father. I needed her to choose me, to rescue me, to walk away from everything for me.

What I saw was her attacking the woman who had shown me more love than anyone else. I saw her fawning over the man who had disrespected me in the worst way. I saw her choosing to get high and live the life instead of staying and fighting for me. She didn't want me. She didn't love me.

Over the years of putting my story into poetry, of sharing with those who've had similar experiences, I've come to realize what hurts me the most about my mother.

It's not the drugs. It's not the irresponsibility. It's not even the lies and broken promises.

Even at forty years old, I don't understand how a woman, any woman, could look at the man who violated her child in a sexual way ever again.

I speak a lot about forgiveness, and I mean every word that I say. Forgiveness, however, does not replace clear fundamental values. I am her daughter, carried in her womb, birthed through her canal, blood and flesh of her own body. She's always claimed to love me more than anyone in the world, has argued me down about how much I mean to her. Yet, from the time I reconciled with my father, she has fallen back into a sexual relationship with him over and over again.

This may sound hypocritical to some, and I can understand that. Imagine a little girl, though. A little girl that had her entire life flipped upside down in ways she couldn't understand. Imagine her being taught the gravity of the things that happened to her. Imagine the words that were used to describe it. *Dirty. Nasty. Dog. Filthy.* Imagine her figuring out how those words applied to her; and then imagine her watching her mother in the arms of the man that introduced those words into her life. Imagine this little girl watching her mother kiss him. Watching her mother swoon at the sight of him. Watching her mother melt into his arms like he's the only man on the earth.

As I write these words, I know that I am still that little girl. Despite my growth and maturity in other areas, my heart still breaks at the thought that she could still want him. To be touched by him. That she wasn't repulsed by him.

In my head, I'm allowed to deal with this anyway I need to. They were the parents. They betrayed me. They hurt me. They slacked on their God-given responsibilities to protect me and keep me from harm. So, *I* decide, *I* get to choose. I get to say '*yes, you can be in my life*' or '*I don't want to have anything to do with you*'.

Her choice, her only choice should have been *me*.

This still hurts in a way that is difficult to put into words. On one hand, I feel selfish, like a hypocrite, like I don't have a right to this pain. I feel like I should understand that Ileene also has a story, that she has pain and voids that were never filled. That maybe this was the best she could do.

When I go through her story, however, I get myself right up to the point where she took back to his bed, and that spoils it for me. That is the point of no return, the line that never should have been crossed. She doesn't know it, but that   is   where   she   finally   lost   me.

Over the years, I have tried on numerous occasions to have a relationship with my mother. I've sent for her, let her live with me, paid her bills, cussed people out about her, gone looking for her when Granny was scared for her life. I even tried to foster an environment where she could have a relationship with my children. No matter what, she always seemed to do something that reminded me that she couldn't be trusted with my heart.

I started singing professionally in 1999. I was recording, hosting and performing in shows, winning contests and scouting talent for an independent record label in Detroit. We sold so many cd's out of the trunk, that we planned a record release party.

My label planned this huge party for me, complete with DJ, food and drinks. We sold tickets for a few weeks before the event. I may not have been a household name, but I was a known name on the local scene, and the party sold out. Of course, I invited my friends, family, classmates, and fellow artists. Everyone was welcome, even my mom.

At the time, she was living in a flat that had originally been mine. She had recently moved back to the city after living in Florida. She'd called and said she was coming home and needed somewhere to stay. In those days, I couldn't help getting excited when she came around. Even though she had always let me down, I desperately wanted a relationship with her, so I agreed that she could stay with me. In true Ileene fashion, there was more to the story. When she got there, she wasn't alone. She pulled up with her boyfriend. Caught off guard, I watched as they both brought bags into my house. We never discussed this. She never asked if it was okay. They just moved in. She had this sense of entitlement that still baffles me to this day. It wasn't long before we were fighting, sometimes violently, and after one particularly nasty fight, I decided to leave my house. Rather than put my mother on the street, I moved into the house of the guy I was dating (against my better judgement) and left everything I owned for her.

Anyway, I spoke to her leading up to the release party, and even the day of. She promised that she was coming. I was skeptical but decided to give her the benefit of the doubt. She liked to pretend that she had taught me how to sing and acted like we were so close when in public, so I figured she wouldn't miss a chance to be introduced as Lady Queen's mother.

She never showed up.

In contrast, my holier-than-thou grandmother, who didn't let anyone see her doing anything, bought out two tables and had almost the entire church in attendance at the club. See, that was the difference. Granny, who was totally against me singing 'worldly' music, supported me in every possible way, and made sure everyone else supported me. She even went by my old apartment that day to pick my mother up, so she could have no excuses, but there was always something with Ileene.

I could give so many examples, but ultimately, they all lead to the same conclusion. My mother was unable to get over herself long enough to get to me. She missed my record release. She missed the births of my children. She didn't come to my college graduation. She didn't come to my wedding because she was mad that Granny was walking me down the aisle. I'm convinced the only reason she made it to my high school graduation is because she was living in the house with us at the time. She's never shown up for me like I needed her to.

What makes it worse is that Granny raised me to respect her anyway, so whenever she needed something, I showed up for her. I won't lie and say that I wasn't disrespectful, that I didn't tell her exactly how I felt in no uncertain terms. I yelled. I screamed. I cursed.

But I ALWAYS showed up.

CHAPTER 13

Continuing my attempt to be fair throughout this book, I must add that about twenty years ago, my mother was diagnosed with bipolar disorder, PTSD, dissociative personality disorder, and I have no clue what else. She has alcohol and substance abuse issues. In fact, as I write these words, she is currently in a treatment center. She also has a multitude of physical health issues that plague her body.

I include these things because it can be said that perhaps the reason why my mom has lived such a hard life, or the reason why she's incapable of being the mother I need her to be, is because she has these chemical imbalances. Mental illness is real, and I don't take it lightly or minimize the havoc it can wreak in the lives of those affected.

Logically, all of this make sense, and although I have my skepticisms, I do believe she suffers from some mental illness. Hell, most people suffer from some mental illness. The problem is that I don't view all of this through logical lenses. All the logic in the world can't quiet the tears of the six-year-old little girl standing in that hallway. It won't erase the sound of the words that broke me. All the research I've done, all of the therapists I've met with, all of the diagnoses in the world can't explain the pain of the little girl standing on the stairs, being rejected by the person she wanted the most.

Over the years, I've learned how to cope, how to quiet the screams of that little girl. I moved on with my life. I had children of my own in which I could pour all of the love, protection and devotion that I missed. I made it my business to be better than her. That was how I measured myself. If I loved them more than she loved me. If I was there for them. If I never left them. If I gave them what they needed. If they never looked at me the way I look at her.

I was living in the prison of my pain. Everyday trying to outrun a phantom. To be better than someone that I never had to compete with. Because of this, I always came up short. It was never enough. I was never good enough. I didn't accomplish enough. Nothing wiped the pain away. I spent every waking moment trying not to become Ileene, completely oblivious to the fact that I was just like her. She spent her life trying to prove Granny wrong. Trying to prove that she could be a good mother. Trying to prove that she was a good daughter. Trying to prove that her faults were the result of those things which had been done to her or taken away from her. She lived in the prison of her pain. I am my mother's daughter.

As an adult now, it is hard for me to believe that we will ever have a true mother - daughter relationship. She doesn't bring me comfort. She doesn't know how to talk to me, how to interact with me. She desperately wants to be a part of my world, but I'm not sure if I have the capacity to make room for her. She still struggles with her addictions. She still lies. She still stirs up trouble. She still contends that the world is against her. She lives in a constant state of victimization, and that is so far removed from the world I've tried to create for myself. I've been through a lot yes, but I'm nobody's victim. Life has been what it is, and I've done my best to move along its rocks and waves. Sometimes I make it, sometimes I don't, but each time, I get up and I try again.

I will never abandon her, though. I don't know how to do that. She would probably disagree and say that I've already abandoned her because I won't let her live with me, or when she asks for money I won't give it. That's not how I define abandonment. Those are barriers. Over the years, I've learned what I can and can't accept from her, what hurts too much, what angers me beyond repair. I've learned how to fit my mother within the boundaries of my life, and it may not be what she wants, but it's what works for me. When I see that she is truly trying to help herself, I step in. I make calls and reach out on her behalf in ways that I never allow her to see. I don't speak with her every day, but I have set times that I look for her, make sure she's alive. People know to call me if something happens to her. When I'm able, I buy her groceries, or gas, though I will not give her money. She cannot live with me, but if I feel in my heart that she's clean and not using, I will break my neck to find her a place to stay. I'll never tell her all the calls I really make, the people I talk to, the prayers I pray on her behalf. She doesn't need to know. The same woman that she despised for so many years because of me taught me certain principles that I'll never walk away from.

I'm not sure my mother will ever understand how much it was really all about her. How I longed for her. How I needed her. Fathers are great and yes, we need them, but children look for mommy first. When they scrape their knee, they cry for mommy. When they fall off their bike, they yell for mommy. When a girl experiences her first heartbreak, it's mommy she wants. The first time a woman finds out she's pregnant, it's mom she rushes to call. When a young woman gets raped for her eighteenth birthday, it's mom she needs by her side.

Whether intended or not, my mom has been a constant source of pain, disappointment, anger and grief. She's lied on me and to me. She's made up stories and told them to people in my life that caused major rifts and huge disagreements. She's broken promises. She's broken my heart. Worse? Repeatedly, she's forgotten, or claimed to have forgotten doing these things all while starting the process over again.

There is one thing that I know for sure, God is the God of the impossible. I cannot rule out a major shift in my mother's life. I will never say that she can't be freed from her bondage. Our relationship, our story, is just another reason why writing this book was so important to me. Understanding that there are so many daughters that need their mothers. So many mothers that miss their daughters. So many women reliving stories of the past and birthing those stories into their children. I love my mother. I want what's best for her. I want her to be happy and whole. I want the latter years of her life to be greater than the former. I want her to take back what the enemy stole from her. I want her to want these things for herself.

I will always show up...

INTERLUDE: LADY QUEEN

Directly out of high school, I enlisted in the United States Air Force. Granny was not happy and Auntie Madie was very disappointed, but I was tired of school. More so, I just wanted to get away. The travel opportunities and hierarchy structure of the military sounded like a way out, and I had honestly been looking for an escape route all of my life. I tried to appease them by saying that enlisting would ensure that my education was paid for later, but in the end, I think they knew I just wanted to go. I love my family because although the majority of them did not agree, they were very supportive (in front of me at least).

Unfortunately, during training, my asthma returned making it impossible for me to complete the requirements, and I was granted a medical discharge. I was devastated, and somehow made up in my mind that I was a failure. My parents had both successfully gone into the service, and I couldn't even do that. Once I got the asthma back under control, I got a little job at a copy shop downtown and decided it was time I had my own place. I loved Granny to death, but she had too many rules, and like most new adults, I was ready to do what I wanted to do without restriction. I didn't move far, only one street over in fact. My cousin stayed in a four-family flat around the corner from us, and the unit upstairs was available. It was perfect. Close enough that I could go home to eat and shop in Granny's cabinets and far enough away that I could party and have company without her watchful gaze.

The next few years turned out to be the best of my young adult life. This was my first taste of freedom. The first Sundays that came and went without me going to church. The first time I spent the night with my boyfriend (without sneaking). The first time I hosted a party, invited whomever I wanted, and watched it rock into the wee hours of the morning. The first time I was truly responsible for my own bills and welfare. The first time I felt like a real adult.

My flat became party central. Friends, co-workers, cousins, siblings, even strangers were invited. As long as they brought what I was drinking and what they were drinking they could get in. Some nights were mellow, and some nights were raunchy, but all of them were fun. Things were a lot different back then. Everyone looked out for each other. My younger sister and cousins and I were surrounded by guys, but no one tried to take advantage of us. No one disrespected us or hurt us. To the contrary, the guys in our circle were very protective, and ensured that any outsiders followed whatever invented protocol they set, and we never had a problem. Well, outside of driving my ninety-year-old landlord nuts.

From riding up my street spread eagle in a mini skirt on the hood of a T-Top Monte Carlo, to ripping off my cute white dress and throwing up on my living room floor during one of my parties, I lived like there was no tomorrow. This was my taste of freedom. The longest time spent without the mask. In this environment, in my own space, I was truly the Queen, and I loved every second of it.

Although the parties were fun, many of my nights were spent nursing a glass of Boone's Farm on my living room floor. Alone, surrounded by stacks of buy-one-get-ten-free compact discs from mail order music clubs like BMG and Columbia, I no longer had to record the lyrics of my favorite songs off of the radio. I could read them from the cd liner, cry my tears, and feel my emotions all night long, and I did. I started to remember how good singing felt. How much of a release it was, how much freedom it provided. Lauryn Hill, Boyz To Men, TLC, Dru Hill, Whitney Houston, Luther Vandross, Earth, Wind and Fire, The Ohio Players. Music became the cloud on which I rested my head.

I began to write again, to turn my poetry into melody. My quest for love came back full force, but this time it came from my diaphragm. I inhaled my pain and exhaled my misery. I released my shame in long, practiced notes, with precise breath control and natural vibrato. I sang into hair brushes and empty pop bottles. I filled notebooks with lyrics and hooks. I decided that this was my future, my calling.

While working in the copy center at a law firm downtown, I met a young, African American female attorney named MJ. MJ was a rising star amidst the old boy's club, and when I reached out for help she willingly agreed. The first time I sang for her, it was after-hours at the firm and we were in her office. I closed my eyes and sang something I'd written, completely losing myself in the melody, forgetting we were in an office building and that I had a big mouth. When I finished and opened my eyes, MJ was staring at me in awe.

"Queen! Why didn't you tell me you could sing like that?"

I just shrugged with a sheepish grin, and our friendship was forged in stone from that day on. MJ became my entertainment attorney, taking me to meetings, introducing me to producers and other people she knew in the industry. I sang for an up and coming producer from the south, and he was blown away, and immediately wanted to sign me to his company. While MJ was going over the contracts, she took me to another studio, and had me sing for the owner of a local independent label, K-Lew Entertainment. He also wanted to sign me, and well, let's just say things got interesting between the two companies. A couple of meetings, a few arguments and a bar brawl later, I signed with K-Lew, and became the First Lady of K-Lew Entertainment.

K-Lew and I brought out the best in each other creatively. Our musical chemistry was crazy! Whenever I had a session, he brewed my special tea, had the overhead lights off, and the candles burning. I'd spend a couple minutes listening to whatever new track he'd done throughout the week, and then I'd grab my pencil and my notebook. There was no mask here, no identity search. It was just me and the music, the pulse of the bass, the flight of the strings, and the words floating in front of my eyes. The sound. Although I was surrounded by music, equipment, and sometimes a room full of people, I was alone with my heart, alone with my fears, alone with whomever I had become. When I stood in front of the mic, I poured out every part of me that I'd been holding for years. Lady Queen was born.

K-Lew nicknamed me 'Queen One-Time' because I almost never made mistakes. If we did another take, it was because we wanted to, not because I'd forgotten the words or missed a que. I was in my zone, and I never wanted to leave. We sometimes spent days in the studio writing and recording. Eventually the other artists on the label figured out that I was a writer and good at arranging, so it wasn't long before I was invited to everyone's sessions. The rappers grew protective of me, and we were one huge family. I sang hooks for them, they spit verses for me, we made history in that studio, and I was blessed to stand with some of the greatest talent in Detroit.

We had so much local success with my first album that we all quit our day jobs and pursued music full time. I won contests all over the city. We hosted our own open mic night. We popped up anywhere our tinted-out trucks could fit and sold CDs, the guys selling to the women and me selling to the men. People would stick the album in their car radios before purchasing, sometimes so impressed that they drove off having purchased two or three. We were living it up and loving every new opportunity that came our way.

The greatest of those opportunities was getting a call from *The Jenny Jones Show*. We mailed the album out to several record companies and tv shows in the hopes that someone would hear it and give us a call. Not only had they heard it, but they wanted me to come and compete in the *2000 Jenny Jones Battle of the Bands*, a music competition the show hosted every year for all genres of music. We were stoked. Forty million viewers! We would finally get the type of recognition we'd been working for.

Needless to say, that trip to Chicago was a wonderful experience. Tamar Braxton was the special guest performer on the show that day, an unexpected treat. While the other performers were practicing dance steps in the halls and doing runs in the green room, I sat quietly, focused on my goal, and waiting on my turn to take the stage. Granny had always taught me *'be ye also ready'*, so I felt if I didn't have it by then, I never would. When Jenny Jones called my name and I took the stage, I just did what came naturally. I didn't have a complicated dance routine, my outfit was cute but simple, and nothing about me was flashy. It was just me, the music, and the crowd, the way it always was.

I walked off the stage that day with the winning trophy for the R&B category in my hands, and it was validation that all of our hard work had paid off. Back in Detroit the phone started ringing, the appearances started pouring in, and Lady Queen was on the rise. We started recording the second album, with every intention of following the same formula that had worked the first time. There was one major difference though; Lady Queen was trying to follow her dream, but Queen had fallen in love.

PART THREE:
MRS. NELSON

My Eye

The existence of my mind's eye
The persistence of my blind eye
Causes me to hear nothing
And see only what I choose
Otherwise I have much too much to lose
My heart aches for the fallacy that is you
My soul yearns for the heartbreak that is you
I can't condition myself to go
But I can't convince myself to stay
So what do I do?
The existence of my mind's eye
The persistence of my blind eye
Causes me to ignore the words you speak so clear
To misjudge the signs that hang so near
To me
I want to be alone
I don't want that
I'm too selfish
It's not you, that
Causes me to be this way
Yet it's still not okay
The existence of my mind's eye
The persistence of my blind eye
Causes me to overlook the eminent pain
To only see what I want to gain
I hold on to the words you say when
You're deep inside of me
Even though those words can hold
No true meaning, but

I make them good enough
I will them strong enough
Cuz my love alone can change it right?
Cuz my heart in its whole can make it right...
The existence of my mind's eye
The persistence of my blind eye
Oh how it hurts to look at my reality
How the bitter truth stings with totality
My need to be yours is overwhelming
It overpowers me
To be yours, to be held, to be...loved
That illusion eludes me
The existence of my mind's eye
The persistence of my blind eye
Inevitably, it's just not in the cards for me
The head over heels, the picket fences
The gigantic solitaires, the perfect senses
Happiness defined is but a love denied
Better to have loved than have lost
But is it better to lose when love remains?
Is it better to walk away when hurt reigns?
How did the ancestors do it?
How on earth did they make it through it?
I'm doing bad y'all, feel like I'ma fall y'all
Into the loveless pits, the bowels of the endless drifts
The cry my soul emits...
The existence of my mind's eye
The persistence of my blind eye
I can feel my heart being ripped from its core
I can feel my lungs breathing no more
I can touch the drops of my soul that have escaped

The pieces of my being being raped
Nothing but a skeleton, nothing but emptiness
You took a chunk outta my spirit like Eliot Ness
You were untouchable, but I was a fool
I reached out anyway and tried to touch you
I grabbed and I grabbed
Foolishly, I thought I had you
But it was all a facade
You pulled a David Copperfield
Cuz when I opened my hand
It was empty, and my scars still haven't healed
I know it's time to let you go
I know I need to heal and grow
But dammit, I really wanted you
I had so much shit for us to do
All is not fair in love,
Nothing could be farther from the truth
And until the end of forever
I will unconditionally love you...
Fighting the existence of my mind's eye
With the persistence of my blind eye

~Shaquenia Nelson - Post Divorce~

CHAPTER 14

The years of my life covered in this book shaped the woman I would become, the decisions I would make, and the mistakes that changed my life. My early years taught me lessons that it would take decades to unlearn: that I had to please in order to be loved; that anger equals abandonment; that I had to suppress my true feelings to keep people in my life; that it was okay to change who I am if it meant they wouldn't leave me. Unfortunately, it also taught me that the real me was incapable of being loved, and that I had to take whatever was dished out to me.

I'd spent my entire life hunting an identity that I didn't even understand.

When I was about twenty-one years old, I met and fell in love with the man who would become my first husband, let's call him Jackson. Jackson was friends with my step-sister's boyfriend and had been to a couple of the parties that I'd thrown. I remember thinking he was cute and funny, and I loved the way he carried himself, full of confidence like he owned the world. Initially I played him because I wasn't sure if he sold dope or not, and that was where I drew my bad boy line, but it wasn't long before I asked my sister about him. He came to my house on Christmas Eve and we sat in my basement talking for hours. I was pleasantly surprised at how intelligent he was, how articulate and well spoken. I knew he had a reputation though, so I didn't expect to fall for him. I was just bored that night and looking for some attention, but the joke was on me. The following week was the New Year, and Jackson had a huge party at his house. I was at home with my family celebrating in our usual fashion when there was a knock on the door. Jackson was standing there with two bottles of Moet for me and my family. He stayed long enough to have a toast with us, give me a kiss, and head back to his party that was in full swing. This dude who garnered all this respect in the streets, left his party to drive from the westside all the way to the eastside just to have a toast with me after only one week? All you needed was a box of crackers to go with the cheese on my face.

In those early days, Jackson made it all about me. No matter what he had going on, he never missed an opportunity to make me feel special. We had couples only nights at his house, where Jackson would cook, and we'd play cards, and he made sure no one smoked around me because of my asthma. We had certain weeknights where he would shut everyone else out and lay with me while we watched our favorite television shows. Even the times when he came in at three or four in the morning, waking me up with a chicken pita from Coney Island and a pint of cognac, were special to me. Jackson managed to touch the little girl places in me that no one else noticed. The places that longed to feel loved and protected, the places that needed to belong to someone. I loved going out with Jackson because I never worried about anything happening to me. He commanded respect wherever we went, and because I was his babe, respect was given to me. I finally felt safe. I had been chasing these feelings all of my life and almost overnight, Jackson delivered them to me.

Don't get it twisted though, Jackson was definitely a 'bad boy'. A 'street nigga'. He was nothing I needed and everything I wanted. From our first date, he had his hooks in me, and I gladly left them in. Like every other relationship in my life, I learned who I needed to become to make him love me. I tried to figure out what he liked, what he hated, what he wanted, what he needed. I tried to be everything I thought he longed for. *Mask On.*

The problem with trying to be someone you're not is that eventually, the real you keeps popping out. Don't get me wrong, I loved Jackson, and I know he loved me the best that he knew how, but there was no way our relationship could be happy and healthy. I wanted him to change into my idea of a knight in shining armor, and I tried to change into his damsel. He was content with who he was, and knew exactly which direction he was headed, so why would he change? I was the one with identity issues. I was the one looking for him to supply me with those things I should have been able to find within myself.

It was good at first. Late night sex, drinks and talks. Sharing of dreams. We bonded over our love of music, both of us writers and performers. I wanted desperately to fit into his world, but I didn't, and he didn't fit into mine, so I created a new world. Of course, I wouldn't listen to anyone. The more my family and friends tried to talk to me about the changes they saw in me, the more I rebelled. I don't remember when I realized that I was afraid of him, but even that didn't deter me.

My family thought I'd lost my mind. I barely spoke to most of my friends, at least not the ones who'd known me most of my life. I made new friendships with people who only new this recreated Shaquenia. The girl with the mask on. It's important to note that Jackson didn't stop me from seeing my friends or try to control my movements. These were decisions that I made on my own, either consciously or subconsciously. I was content with waiting on Jackson to get home because I knew when he got there, it would be all about us. The friends that had grown up with me didn't fit into this world, didn't know this girl, and I didn't want to explain or pretend. So, I buddied up with the girlfriends of his friends, women that were living similar lives, women that wouldn't question the mask I wore because they would never even see it.

After about two years, I was pregnant with our first child, and that sealed it in stone for me. No way was I going to allow my baby to go through life without two parents. No way would my baby be raised in a single parent home or wonder where mommy or daddy was. I would prove everyone wrong. I would be the one to break the chain. I would create the family I never had. We were in this thing for life. I was never letting him go, and he was never getting away from me.

I had been singing and recording most of our relationship, but when I found out I was pregnant, I didn't feel as though the life I was living would be conducive to raising a child. Late nights at the studio, drinking and smoking cigars with the rappers, performances and appearances almost every night. We were so busy that at one point my family staged an intervention. I lost a large amount of weight because of the studio hours, lack of sleep and unusual eating habits we all had. Granny, Auntie Madie and one of the church members came to the studio with a cooler full of Boost nutritional drinks, peanut butter crackers and trail mix. Granny thought I was doing drugs and came to have prayer and feed me back to health. Although we all cracked up once they left, (it took some time to convince them that I wasn't a crackhead), they were right that I wasn't taking care of myself like I should've been. As soon as I found out about the baby, I knew it was time to put my dream down and become a responsible adult.

During my pregnancy, Jackson and I broke up several times, and he began a relationship with another woman. I was devastated. Only a woman can describe how once you're carrying a man's baby, you long for him in ways you never thought possible. You want his arms around you. You are soothed by the sound of his voice. You imagine which features the baby will get from both of you. You want to be under him, and to be the most important thing in his world. Imagine having all these feelings while thinking of him with someone else. Wondering who he's holding, touching, loving.

The night I went into labor was one of the scariest of my life. It was the day before my due date, and I had just left the doctor with instructions that the baby could come at any time. Granny took me to Taco Bell and we went home. After our last breakup, Granny told me to get my stuff from Jackson's house and move back home. From that point on, she became my 'baby daddy', taking me to every single appointment, feeding me crab legs and watermelon and whatever else I wanted, and becoming the 'guardian of the belly', not allowing any strangers to rub, touch, or barely even look at my stomach. She went from being totally disappointed in me to completely overprotective of me almost overnight, and I was grateful for her support.

The pains started around seven that evening, and I immediately called the hospital. I spoke to the nurse, told her my symptoms, and she told me to call back in an hour. An hour later, I had seen the mucus plug, the pain was worse, and I was certain that it was time to go. I called the nurse back. She told me this was wonderful news, and to call her back in an hour. For the rest of the night, every hour on the hour, the nurse cooed to me, assured me everything was right on schedule, and instructed me to call her back in an hour. I was certain that she was crazy, some nut from the psych floor that had stolen a badge and some scrubs and decided to play on the phones, but Granny told me to follow her directions. Around six the next morning, Nazi Nurse finally gave us clearance to come to the hospital, and Granny, who had barely slept a wink, grabbed my bag, my hand, and rushed me to Hutzel Hospital.

With Granny, Jackson, my dad, my step-mom, my siblings (all of them), a couple of my friends, and all the medical staff, the delivery room was a madhouse. It was now my official due date, and although I was contracting hard as hell, I had not dilated at all. Hours passed, and the pain intensified, but there was still no movement. This baby was not ready to meet the world. Granny's proclamation that the baby was in my belly getting her hair and nails done to be cute for her arrival was met with a death stare that could rival Cyclops in any battle. At three that afternoon, the doctor decided to induce labor, and the already intense contractions tripled in severity. I was tired. I was ready for it all to be over. I needed some help. *Mask On.*

Suddenly, the activity in my room quieted. My family, who had been joking and light hearted before, was now quiet and whispering. I heard my step-mom whisper to my dad,

"She's so quiet. She's not making a sound. I thought she'd be screaming."

Granny walked past, dabbing her eyes with a crumpled tissue, and I heard her say,

"I've never seen her in so much pain. I hate that I can't do anything for her. I wish I could fix it."

I'll never forget those words. The declaration that even in her disappointment in the fact that I was about to be an unwed mother, she still loved me enough to want to ease my pain. I never mentioned it, but her words gave me a strength she'd never know. For another twelve hours, my only displays of pain were the tears streaming from my eyes; the grip of the hospital bed as I tried to rearrange my position whenever a contraction hit; the deep breaths I forced myself to take each time my stomach hardened, and I felt the pull of pain from my back to my abdomen. What my family couldn't understand was that I was a master at dealing with pain, at leaving my body, at pretending I was someone else, somewhere else, feeling something different. That night the mask didn't save me from the pain, but it gave me the strength to endure it.

From the contractions that started on Monday evening, my gorgeous baby girl didn't make her debut until three forty-five Wednesday morning. As soon as I saw her face, I forgot about all the pain. Head full of jet-black curly hair, huge bright brown eyes, pale chalky white skin, and chubby kissable cheeks. She was beautiful, and she was mine. My heart exploded with a feeling that was unfamiliar to me. The mask now floated just out of my reach, and I prayed that with her, I wouldn't need it.

Once Jackson saw our baby girl, for a short time he wanted to be a family again. He held her, looked at me in amazement, stared at her in awe. He was gentle with me, loving. I saw in his face the love that had once been. I didn't ask any questions, I just accepted him back into my life and started the process over. This time, however, there was a difference. Something in me changed when I held my daughter for the first time. When I looked into her eyes and realized that she was depending on me, that she needed me, that without me, she wouldn't make it, I grew up. That was the scariest day of my life. The day I realized that it was no longer about me. That I no longer mattered. That I could not fail. I didn't mean to, but I put the mask back on, this time out of fear.

As badly as I wanted to be married and have the perfect picket fence family, it was never going to work because I didn't know who I was. I had created a version of me that I thought I could live with. Actually, I created several versions of me. I became whoever anyone needed me to be. This was not a decision that I made consciously, but a trait that I developed when my identity was stolen from me. I didn't know who to be. I'd grown up confused. Everything about how I was born was wrong, or dirty. So, with Granny and most of my family, I was Queenie. With my friends I was Monie, or Shaq or Queen. With my fans, I was Lady Queen. At church, I was Sis. Witherspoon, or Sis. Irving's granddaughter. Later, I became 'their mother' or 'his wife.

As long as I could be anybody to someone, I never had to be anyone to me.

Reflection

It was late one night
And my soul cried the blues
I looked all around me
And I had nothing to lose
How exactly did I get here?
When did I fail?
When did I become so useless?
So invisible, so frail?
Didn't I have a future?
Wasn't I the joy and pride?
Didn't they all love me?
Weren't they all on my side?
But what happened?
And then...I remembered...
I turn to the right, I look down
And...I remembered.
I remember why all the pills surround me
I remember why the blades are on the table
I remember that I've broken all the rules
And that my life is no longer a fable
I pull the covers around her
And I wonder what kind of mother I might have been
If I just had the strength to hold on to her
If I could only make amends
But I have nothing to offer her
I can be of no example
I'm no better than the next girl
I'm not even a pure sample

I really love this baby
God knows I do
But to expose her to an undeserved life
Is nothing short of child abuse
So...I wipe my tears, and...
I make up my mind
I've just got to do it
She's better off, she'll be alright
The family will get her through it
I pick up the first bottle
I'm ready to go
But as my hand reached my lips
The Lord said, "NO!!
IN MY WAY, THERE IS ALWAYS A WAY
IN ME, THERE'S ALWAYS DELIVERANCE
DON'T BE SO QUICK TO GIVE UP
I GAVE YOU INTELLIGENCE, NOT IGNORANCE
DIDN'T I GIVE YOU A BRAIN?
WELL WHY HAVE YOU FORGOTTEN TO USE IT?
LOOK TO THE HILLS FROM WHENCE COMETH YOUR
HELP
I GAVE YOU A CHOICE, NOW CHOOSE IT!!!!"
So, I don't know why, but I picked up the line
And dialed my aunt on the phone
With divine intervention, I didn't even think
Somehow, I just knew she'd be home
I said, "T, this is my last chance
I just can't take it anymore
I've got to get away from this place
Go to school, make a life, do some more!"
She said, "Baby, don't worry, I've got you

You just decide where you want to go
Now make some calls and do some research
And when you're ready to go, we'll go!"
Well, that's how it all started
That was the first day of the rest of my life
With honors I graduated from that college
And I came home to start a new life
So don't ever forget where you come from
And I'm not talking about your hood or your street
I'm talking about your heavenly residence
The place where the heavens and the earth meet
And remember that with HIM you can do ANYTHING
Even if the path seems too steep
You just trudge through the mud and keep moving
Ask him to help you if it gets too deep
On that night I had no way of knowing
That I'd be standing here today
Baring my soul before you
Telling you that the LORD can make a way
But GOD knew, in fact, he was preparing me
My every mistake was made with a purpose
I know that he wanted to save me
Because I certainly didn't deserve this
So when life pierces you with its daggers
Holds you down and renders you helpless
Lift your sword of salvation, stand tall
And let GOD handle the rest!!

~Shaquenia Witherspoon - Postpartum~

CHAPTER 15

By the time Arionna was seven months old, reality had set in. I was a single mother, working minimum wage, taking care of a newborn alone, with no outlook for a future. Jackson and I, once again broken up, were on terrible terms. Granny helped me get an apartment in her building, and did as much as she could, but each day, I continued to feel more and more overwhelmed. I didn't see a scenario where my baby and I lived happily ever after. Regardless of how badly we argued and disagreed, I still loved Jackson, and was distraught that our little family was torn apart. Late at night while she was sleeping, I would whisper to Arionna, apologizing for messing up her life, for not being able to keep her family together. For being a failure.

I began to think that she was better off without me. What did I have to offer her? No money, no picket fence, no family. I was setting her up for a life of sadness, just like mine, and I didn't want that for my baby. I watched her sleep, tears streaming down my face, and I knew that I didn't deserve her. I knew that she deserved a better life, a better chance, a better mom.

One night, I sat in the living room that doubled as my bedroom in our studio apartment. All around me was every medicine bottle I could find. The Motrin prescribed to me for my cramps. Imitrex for my migraines. Valium for muscle spasms. Cough syrup with codeine left over from a bout with bronchitis. Some random arthritis medicine that Granny had forgotten. A pint of cognac for good measure. It seemed very simple.

I began to pour the pills into my hand, stealing glances at my sleeping daughter in the bassinet next to me. The front of my shirt was soaked before I even realized I was crying.

It may not seem like it now, but it's better this way, I pleaded with her silently.

You'll have a better life. I'm sorry I messed it all up. Maybe I should've kept singing. Maybe I should've just gone to school...

So many times in my life people have asked me how I know that God is real. I don't have long thesis statements or drawn out hermeneutic explanations. What I have are undeniable moments where God has made Himself known to me. This was one of those moments. I know He stepped in to save me from myself. I wasn't at all wavering in my decision to end my life, but instantly, my calm reserve left me. Suddenly, I could no longer see the hand holding the pills, but it began to shake, and the pills began to fall. My entire body was shaking, racking with sobs. The tears streaming from my eyes mixed with the snot pouring from my nose and it all landed in a mess on my shirt. I slid from the futon to the floor, no strength left, my stomach clenched in a soundless scream. The room was spinning, and suddenly I felt the urge to call Auntie Madie.

I don't remember picking up the phone, or dialing her number, but when I heard my aunt's voice, the screams started. I couldn't form any words, all I could do was scream, and cry, and scream some more. It all came tumbling out, the pain, the fear, the disappointment. Once she got me to confirm that the baby was fine, Auntie Madie just let me scream. This woman had the patience of Job, and I'm sure a reinforced heart, otherwise, she would've died of a heart attack.

"I can't do this," I sobbed when I could finally get words out.

"Can't do what?"

"Any of it. I can't raise this baby. I can't be a single mom. I can't give her a good life. I can't do this by myself. I'm tired. I can't do this. I just wanna go. Please. I just wanna go!"

"Ok. Where do you want to go?" Not the response I expected. For years my aunt had tempered my storm with her calm. I should have known this would be no different.

"I--I--If I can't go to school, then I just want to die. Just let me die!" No clue where that came from. School? Five minutes ago, I was ready to end it all, now I was ready to be a college student? What just happened here?

"No problem. I'll tell you what, decide where you want to go, and we'll apply. Simple."

"But it's APRIL! It's way past all of the deadlines for financial aid and college applications. There's no way I can go to school. Plus, what am I gonna do with the baby?" I knew I had her with that one.

"Just look and call me back." I hung up the phone totally confused on what had just transpired. Staring at the pills that had fallen on the floor, the fog cleared. I began to understand that God had just saved my life.

Thirty minutes later, Auntie Madie called back and gave me the web address for Ferris State University and told me they had family housing for students with children. She never wavered in her confidence that I could get in, regardless of the deadlines and any other excuses I could come up with. When I saw the campus, the townhouses for families and the different programs offered, I felt the first spark of hope I'd had in a long time. Maybe I really could do this.

Four months later, Arionna and all of our clothes were packed neatly in the back of Auntie's minivan and we were on our way to Ferris. I had been accepted, and although I was too late for family housing, I decided to go anyway and stay in a motel until I could figure something out. I knew that this decision had saved my life, and I couldn't let anything stand in our way.

While we were driving, Auntie said,

"Girl, don't worry. We're gonna get there and they're gonna tell you that someone canceled and hand you a key to a townhouse."

"Ha! From your lips to God's ears!" was my reply.

I guess God was listening because that is *exactly* how it happened. It was another one of those moments where He took the time to show me that He loved me, and that even the small things in my life mattered to Him. All I could do was cry. Auntie just smiled.

"Told ya!"

Ferris was the best thing that happened to me. Still in love with all things creative, I majored in Television and Digital Media Production, and met some of the most talented people in the industry. Because I was already twenty-four years old, I was much older than most of the other students starting the program, and I assumed this would be a barrier. I had never been so wrong. My classmates fell in love with Arionna and were always willing to help me with her. My house became study central, with groups of us gathering to study and do projects, and me cooking for them all and being a mother hen.

School was the reprieve I needed. The magical place where no one knew my history, where they took me exactly as I was, and loved me for it. I excelled semester after semester, always on the Dean's List. I stood with friends and fought for what we believed in. I let them drag me to parties, where I dared to have fun, and laugh into the wee hours of the morning. I wrote, produced, and starred in my first music video, for one of my original songs, and fell in love with the production side of music. I even dated a little, let a couple of young boys and their crushes help me forget about Jackson.

Until the night he called and said, *'I want my family back.'*

Jackson. My kryptonite. My achilles heel. My baby daddy. The one man I had loved more than anyone else since Jay. I had no idea how to deny him. Especially not when he was offering me the one thing my heart still desired. The failure of our family was my greatest regret, and I still wanted Arionna to grow up with both her parents, knowing that she was loved, that we chose her.

It started up gradually at first, with me trying to make it all about the baby, but Jackson knew my weaknesses. He knew how to make me smile, how to show me affection, how to remind me of all the things I loved about him. I would drive home from Ferris on weekends and take Arionna to see him. Well, I wanted to see him, and that was the excuse I used to help justify the trips. Sometimes I'd go and not even let my family know I was in town. I'll never forget the morning I woke up to someone beating on my door on campus. I stumbled down the stairs and opened the door to find Jackson standing there. I was speechless. I didn't know he was coming, in fact, I hadn't spoken to him that week at all. He stayed the entire weekend, took us out, watched movies with us, played games with the baby. His visit took me back to our early days, when he made time for me, when he made it special. I tried to be guarded, to keep Arionna in the forefront, but my heart has always had a mind of its own.

Every time the subject of us getting back together came up, I told Jackson he would have to move up north with us, which he vehemently refused. We were at a roadblock. I was not going to leave school for him and he was not going to move away from Detroit for us. Driving back and forth wasn't that bad in the summer, but Michigan winters could be deadly, and seeing each other wouldn't be an option once the snow hit.

One day out of the blue, Jackson called and asked me to come and get him. It wasn't odd now for him to come and spend the weekend with us, so I asked how long he was staying.

He replied, "I'm staying. We're getting married."

That was my proposal. Jackson never really asked me anything, he always told me, and this was no different.

Although there were plenty of bumps along the way, we eventually got married early the following year, and Jackson did move up north and stay on campus with us. This marriage was my crusade to prove everyone wrong.

See?

My baby daddy married me.

We're a family.

He loves me.

We're gonna make it.

Everything is gonna be just fine.

See?

I got my picket fence.

It ended up being barbed wire...

I will never say that I didn't know who Jackson was. To this day he remains very secure in who he is and who he isn't. He knows what he wants, and what he's willing to do to get it. He also knows what he doesn't want, and what he refuses to deal with no matter what direction it comes from. I've watched him shut down blood family and lifelong friends that have been with him for decades and never look back. I envied that in him, that he knew his value.

I knew exactly what I was getting into. The little girl parts of me wanted every part of Jackson because I saw security there. He was rough around the edges. He was respected in his circle. He didn't necessarily give me the love that I dreamed of, but when he decided to love me, it felt good, and I knew that he was giving me what he could. We spoke different languages, but I was determined to abandon my language and learn his.

There were two barriers to my thought process:

First, although I spent so much time getting to know Jackson so that I could morph into this unknown version of myself, I never stopped to evaluate if I could live with who he really was. I was so busy making myself into who I thought he needed, it never dawned on me that I would have to endure who he was to be with him.

Second, Jackson was much smarter than me. For all his faults and barbaric ways, he saw right through me. He'd grown up in a family very different than mine, and although they'd had their own problems, the areas that I suffered in were foreign to him. I will never tell anyone that Jackson didn't or doesn't love me. I don't believe that. Jackson was just a security blanket at a time when I really needed an alarm system, and had I been a whole, well-rounded young woman, there never would've been a Jackson at all.

Needless to say, ours was a never-ending battle. I wanted him to be something he was not, while also trying to be something I was not, and honestly, in the beginning, I think he was trying to help me figure that out.

CHAPTER 16

Much of our relationship and marriage I won't share for several reasons. Some of it is the same baby mama/baby daddy drama that you hear every day, so there's no need to write yet another story bashing another black man who made some bad choices. Some of it is too hard to share without going into too much of his story, and that's not mine to tell. Some of it, although still painful, would be more harmful than helpful to my children, and that's not the goal.

There is, however, one experience that I have to share because unbeknownst to me, it became a turning point in my life.

I was a newlywed, a recent college graduate, a mother of a five-year-old, and pregnant with my second child. It sounds like the beginning of a fairy tale, but in reality, our marriage was already on the rocks. Jackson was working one week, and unemployed the next. I was about to have a baby, so getting a job was out of the question. The bills were piling up, the arguments were increasing, and the stress was stifling.

Jackson wanted me to shut up and let him do whatever he was gonna do, and I wanted Jackson to sit down and tell me the plan. I was no longer trying to be what he needed, and he was no longer perfect in my eyes. My new objective was taking care of my babies, providing for them, giving them what I never had, being a better mother than I had. It all changed overnight for me. By the time I realized how deep in the hole I'd dug myself, it was much too late, and I was much too loyal to do anything but stay and figure it all out.

I'd recently been on 'punishment' as I call it. In our relationship, that's when Jackson would stop talking to me, sleeping with me, eating with me, or spending time with me. Sometimes he wouldn't come home until six or seven in the morning. He would ignore me like I wasn't there. This particular time, he was upset because I bought a car. Just before I graduated from Ferris, my car died, so when we moved back home I didn't have one. I had bought Jackson a car the previous summer, some old school Lincoln that he wanted, but now I was pregnant and needed a vehicle for me and the children to use. I had used my financial aid refund and tax refund to get us moved back to the city and into a house because he wasn't working at the time. I paid all the deposits, bought all the furniture, did all the things you have to do when you're moving from one city to another. I didn't do it begrudgingly, that was my husband, and we were a family. I just did what needed to be done.

I had a few thousand dollars left and found this Pontiac Grand Am that I wanted. Jackson told me no, he wanted me to buy some Cadillac that he'd found. I hate Cadillacs, and my thought process was I'd done everything that we'd needed, and I should be able to buy the car I wanted since it was for me. He disagreed. I bought my car. He told me that since I was a disobedient wife, then I could figure out how to pay the bills from then on (he'd recently got a job working in a plant). I, of course, had just finished an internship and couldn't work until after the baby was born. He didn't talk to me for over a month, and then just like that, one day he told me to get dressed so we could go get something to eat. These were the types of mind games he played on me. I was pregnant, stressed, worried about everything under the sun, and my husband walked past me every day for a month like I didn't exist. He was a master at turning it on and off. From that day, of course, he started driving my car, the one he didn't want me to buy, and a few weeks later, he crashed it.

By the time I was nine months pregnant with our son, I was exhausted and overwhelmed, but still trying to figure it all out. The baby was laying on my sciatic nerve, so I was on bed rest. Our bedroom was upstairs, so I was forced to sleep in the living room on the couch. I had doctor's appointments weekly to make sure everything was okay, plus I still had an active five-year-old running around and a husband who was never home. Jackson worked nights, would sleep through the morning, and once he got up, he'd hit the door. To add insult to injury, whenever he left, he would jump in my car, and leave that big dumb Lincoln outside, with no concern for what I'd do in case of an emergency. Every time he walked out of the door I wanted to kick a hole in it.

One morning Jackson got up and told me he was going over his best friend's house and would be 'right back'. Hours later, he was still gone and not answering his phone. I was pissed, and although I was only calling to ask him to bring me something from the store, why wouldn't you answer the phone for your pregnant wife in her last trimester at home on bed rest? The more I thought about it, the angrier I became.

Later that day, I was on the phone with my best friends planning the last details of my baby shower. The door opened, and Jackson walked in with his uncle. They were both drunk, and that infuriated me. I knew better than to yell and scream, so I waited for Jackson to go get whatever he was getting, and on his way back out the door (of course he wasn't coming home to stay), I quietly said,

"From now on, drive your own car. Please leave my keys here."

I didn't curse. I didn't scream. I didn't make a scene. I simply made my point. You can go do all the running around with your friends that you want, but if I have an issue here, in this house, with your daughter, carrying your son, I need to be able to get us out of here, since you won't be anywhere around to help me.

He threw my keys on the table, grabbed his and left. That was fine with me, and I went back to my conversation. About twenty minutes later, I heard his car pull up outside, and I thought it strange because I didn't expect him back until after dark.

Jackson stormed into the house, tossed his keys, snatched the phone out of my hand, threw it across the room, and grabbed me around my neck.

I don't know how long it took my brain to catch up with what was happening. What I remember the most is realizing that he wasn't just squeezing my neck, but that he was pressing his thumbs into that little hole, that notch in the base of the neck, the part that crushes your windpipe. That's when I understood that I was choking. That he was squeezing the life out of me. That's when I understood that I was grabbing his hands, fighting, trying to get him to let me go. That the screams weren't coming from me, because I couldn't breathe, but they were coming from our daughter, who was begging him to stop, who was watching, who would remember. That he had pulled me to the floor and I couldn't feel the baby moving inside of me. I kept willing him to move, but he was still. I realized that I couldn't hear, that the room was becoming a vacuum, that everything around me was turning black, that I couldn't hear my daughter screaming anymore...

And just like that, Jackson let me go.

If Jackson spoke during this encounter, I don't remember any of the words. Sometimes, you don't need words to get your point across. I was afraid. I suppose I had always been scared of Jackson in some ways. I'd seen the look in his eyes. He'd backed me into a corner before. Threatened me. I'd heard the stories of those that had come before me. Like most women, though, I believed I would be the exception to the rule.

When he let me go that day, he simply stood and walked into the kitchen. While I was sputtering for air, trying to regain my composure and calm our daughter, Jackson was in the kitchen preparing to fry some fish. It was bizarre.

"Get out" I coughed, through a raw throat.

"I'm not going nowhere" he replied.

I repeated my demand, and he ignored me. My daughter was frantic, refusing to leave my side. The fear in her eyes, pressed me forward. I trudged up the stairs at the risk of endangering my unborn child and grabbed my shotgun out of the closet. For me, it was less about making him leave and more about showing my daughter that this was not okay. Many of you may not understand that, but it's my truth. People are so quick to say what they would or wouldn't do in these situations, but the reality is you have no idea how you will react until you're staring the situation down. In that moment for me, it was about teaching her a lesson. Making sure that she understood it is NOT okay to allow a man to violate you. You do NOT have to sit by and take it. I needed her to see me DO something, right then, in that moment. I needed this to also be a part of her memory of that day. Even in my weakness, in my fear, I made that moment about her and what I felt she needed from me.

With the shotgun in one hand and the phone in the other, I dialed 911. I wasn't foolish enough to believe that my having the gun would scare Jackson. He was from the streets. He could disarm me easily even if I wasn't nine months pregnant and struggling to breathe. It was a no-brainer, but I couldn't think of anything else to do, and my daughter was watching.

"One way or the other, you're gonna leave here tonight," I sputtered.

He listened to my call to the police calmly, while still rinsing the fish in the sink. He wasn't afraid of the police either. In the end, I think it was our daughter that got him to leave. Her tears, her fear. When I hung up the phone, he wiped his hands, grabbed his keys, and just walked out the door.

That night, I put my daughter in the car, we drove to Home Depot and bought new locks, and I let her help me change the locks on our house. We talked about what happened, I tried to secure her, to answer her questions. I tried to explain that daddy loved her, and that sometimes adults make bad choices. I'm not sure if I said any of the right things, but I tried. The next day, she took my wedding ring off my finger and told me not to put it back on. She said that 'daddy was the devil' and we needed to leave him alone.

One week after my baby shower, I let him come back.

It's funny how the mind works. When it happened, I was so determined to show Arionna the right way to handle it, the right way to value herself, the right way to protect herself. Yet, I also used her as the reason for allowing him to return. How was I going to make it with two kids and no job? How could I live with myself if she grew up like I did, wishing she had her parents? Wishing we were a family? How could I face my family and hear *I told you so*? When I set out to prove them all wrong, how could I go back having proved them all right?

I didn't know what to do. This was my husband. We had another baby coming. I needed to figure it out. So, I let him come back, and I learned the next lesson: be quiet and endure the pain of love. Be loyal to the pain. Don't talk about it. There is no escape. Just take it and keep moving.

Six months after our son RJ was born, the kids and I came home, and Jackson was gone.

CHAPTER 17

When Jackson left, there was no pain for me. I was angry, but only for a short time, and only because of the way he left. I had endured everything he'd put me through, stayed when I knew I should have left, embarrassed myself and bit back my pride, and he had the audacity to pack up his stuff and leave me like I'd done something to him? I can laugh at it now, but it wasn't at all funny to me then.

More than anything though, I felt an overwhelming sense of relief. I would have never left Jackson, and God knew that. To this day, I believe that God released me from a situation that I didn't have the strength to leave. A situation that was toxic to my children. A situation that was toxic to my mental and emotional stability. A situation that was slowly choking the life out of me. I had become a totally different person, one that I didn't even recognize, one that I didn't like. I wasn't happy. At the time I blamed Jackson, but it wasn't his fault. I was broken when I met him, and I was broken when he left. Unfortunately, I had now brought two little people into the world through my broken and bruised womb, and there was no way for them to escape unscathed. Jackson, although he was not blameless in what happened inside of our relationship, was not at fault for the person I became, or the expectations that I placed on him that were never his to fulfill.

A few months after Jackson left, I packed up my babies and moved from the city to the suburbs, wanting nothing to do with the memories we had created. I wanted a fresh start, a new beginning. Jackson and I were at odds about almost everything, and I was tired of arguing, tired of being in the same place, tired of pain. After my son was born, I secured a job at a great company, and although I wasn't making an astronomical amount of money, I figured out a way to make it all work. Granny, always my greatest supporter, was a huge help in those days, babysitting whenever I needed her to, cosigning for me a car, giving me money when she could. Auntie Madie and Auntie Mikoe were also huge factors in us getting moved and settled and being there for us.

It was still a struggle though. There was never enough money. Although I had been awarded child support in the divorce settlement, Jackson refused to pay it. We couldn't agree on anything. He wanted to pop up whenever he felt like it and grab the kids, no structure, like most things, he wanted to do it his way. I wanted him to call first, let me know his plan, when he wanted them, and when he would bring them back. He felt I was trying to control him, that he shouldn't have to call or say anything when he wanted to see his kids. So we always ended in a stalemate, and he might not see them at all for weeks or months at a time. It got so bad between us that we couldn't even have a civil conversation. He bought what he wanted for the kids, when he wanted, it was just a mess. We were adults, angry with each other, and the children suffered because of it. There was a lot that we both could have done differently, but we didn't.

In the meantime, I was getting restless. I missed singing, writing and performing. I missed the outlet it afforded me, the relief it provided me, and the therapy it was for me. I had always been a creative, and although I was thriving in the corporate world, my heart wasn't in it. Everything that made me who I was had been suppressed. I wanted more. I wanted Lady Queen back. I wanted the stage. I wanted my notebook. I wanted the microphone and the room full of people. I wanted out.

After a lot of prayer, counseling with my Pastor, and speaking with family, I decided to move to Atlanta. Atlanta had always been a dream for me, but I could never seem to make it happen. Atlanta was mecca to me. In my head, it was the place to be for an upcoming artist. I had family there, and they welcomed me, offering me and my children a place to stay while I got on my feet. This was the biggest decision that I'd ever made because it involved me leaving my comfort zone. I'd never lived my life without Granny, without my church, without my aunt. I'd never truly been on my own, and I wasn't sure I knew how to be. In the end, that is what made the decision for me. I knew that if I didn't grow up before Granny died, I'd never make it in life. I was so connected to her, so rooted in her, that I didn't know anything else. The furthest from her direction I'd gone was to be with and marry Jackson, and even then I relied on her whenever he didn't come through.

I'd spent my life in the comfortable safety of her arms, but it was time for me to fly now. There was a desperation in me that felt if I didn't take this chance, I'd never get another. So,

I made the arrangements with my cousin, left my job, paid my rent for the month, packed up my children, kissed my grandmother goodbye, and headed into the next phase of my life.

CHAPTER 18

There were so many feelings coursing through me the day we left for Atlanta. Tears running down my face, scared but excited, unsure if I could make it on my own seven hundred and fifty miles away from everything that I knew. My stomach bottomed out and I reminded myself to breathe. The further we got from home, the calmer I became. Watching the trees rush past, staring at the lines in the road, catching a glimpse at the occasional horse or cow. I was still in one piece. Granny was behind me, and I hadn't fallen apart, my heart didn't stop beating, my lungs continued to work like they should. Suddenly, I felt free. It was June 8, 2009, and it was the first day of the rest of my life.

I turned to look at my babies, already asleep in the back seat, faces peaceful, mouths drooling, heads bobbing with the movement of the road. We were going to be okay. Things hadn't gone as planned with Jackson, and although I told him I was moving to Atlanta, we hadn't spoken in close to a year. He'd gotten mad one day when he went to pick up our daughter at Granny's house unannounced and she told him he needed to call me first. That enraged him, and he came to my job and caused a scene. My HR dept called the police and I was instructed to file a personal protection order because he made threats against the building. Well, it was granted, and he wasn't allowed contact with the kids for a year. Originally, he'd told me that it wouldn't be a problem for us to move, but of course everything changes when something happens. In fairness, I did not petition the court and ask permission to leave the state. I wasn't sure if we would stay. I didn't give up my apartment or my job right away. I wanted to go for the summer and see what happened. That was technically illegal, and probably unfair to Jackson, but at the time, I also felt like a lot of his actions were unfair as well.

All of this ran through my mind. How I wanted so badly to give them the life they deserved. How sorry I was that I wasn't whole when I had them, that I wasn't complete and by default, they weren't complete. How blessed I felt to have them, how determined I was to make their lives better than anything I'd ever seen in mine. I even made a vow to myself to figure out how to bridge the gap between Jackson and I, so that he could be a part of their lives without all of the friction. We didn't matter, we never would. All that mattered were these two beautiful beings that we'd created, and they deserved the best that we could give them.

For the first time in my life, I felt in control. I'd made a decision for me, on my own. I'd decided how I wanted my future to look and made a move to get there. It was the best feeling in the world. I didn't worry about the fact that I didn't have a job lined up, or a permanent place to stay. I didn't care that I had no set plan or direction. I was moving closer to my goal, and I was confident that I'd made the right choice.

I arrived in Georgia with nothing but bags of clothes and a determination to do something that I'd never done. My cousin and her husband (we'll call them Tiffany and Paul) lived in Lithonia, and they generously offered my family shelter in their home with their two children. Tiffany was on my dad's side, his older brother's step-daughter, but we had met before when they came up north to visit and always remained in touch. As a matter of fact, I had sung at her wedding. When I called her with interest about moving down, she was excited and very helpful. It was a tight squeeze in their small home, but they made us feel welcome, and I was grateful for that.

Tiffany was the type of person that always wanted to help. If you needed a job, she made a list, if you needed a home, she called the realtors, if you had a dream, she grabbed a notebook. She was full of ideas and ready at a moment's notice to lend a hand. Right away she started to help me look for jobs, establish an address, a bank account and a Georgia identity. Besides Tiffany, my God-sister Shaketa also lived in Georgia, and was elated to have me there. She was already looking for apartments for us, determined that I wasn't going back to Michigan...ever.

My first few weeks as a southerner were pretty good. The kids loved the weather and of course being spoiled by everyone, and it felt like we belonged. Shortly after getting there, I answered an ad for an administrative assistant for an entertainment company. Since I was trying to get back into the industry, I figured it would be smart to get close and work my way up. The day of my interview, I pulled into this complex full of homes that literally dropped my jaw.

Parking in front of this huge mansion, I assumed I had hit pay dirt, and I silently thanked God for giving me favor. I got the job and was told I would be working for a major player in the entertainment industry, who had also just been named president over the newly formed film division of a major hip hop brand. (I choose to leave this man and his company nameless because I refuse to give him any publicity one way or the other). Once they found out that my undergrad degree was in Media Production, I was also commissioned to produce a video for a project he was working on. I was so excited, thinking that not only was I in a place that could help me push my music, but I was also getting a chance to work on producing and editing. I called home screaming with excitement and crying tears of joy, telling my family that it was finally happening for me, that my dreams were finally going to come true, that they didn't have to worry about us. I hadn't been in Georgia a full month and things were already taking off.

I should've known that nothing in my life ever works that seamlessly. I realized much too late that this man was running a scheme, not just on me, but on several upcoming artists, making false promises, stealing money, telling lies and fronting for the cameras. What was slated as an administrative assistant position turned into a pyramid scheme of sorts, where we were only paid if we got people to sign up to the 'system'. Once I started producing the video, I worked long, ridiculous hours, often leaving my children with my sister, sometimes not seeing them awake at all in a day. Although I was promised compensation for my work on the video, I never received a dime. A few weeks in, I went to the boss with all of my production sheets, the video, my time sheets, and everything that I'd done up to that point. I'd also done the research on how much I should've been getting paid for my work and explained that although I wasn't asking for that type of compensation, I felt as if I deserved something for my time and effort. He looked at me and laughed. Told me he could call anyone to do what I was doing. He said that my work was garbage, that he didn't need me, that I could leave, that I should be grateful I was there at all. I couldn't believe what he was saying to me because in every edit meeting we'd had about the video, he'd praised my work, told me how great I was doing, and continued to give me more to complete.

Never in my life had anyone devalued my work or work ethic before. I'd always been a prize employee wherever I worked, and his words pierced me to my core. I walked out of his mansion with my head held high, but by the time I got to my car, I deflated like an undercooked soufflé. I had just left my cousin's home and moved into a new apartment. I had told my family and friends that I was in ATL doing big things, because I honestly believed I was. I had no other form of income and no help. What was I going to do now?

Suddenly, every disappointment that I'd ever felt came crashing down on me. I'd failed as a daughter. I'd failed as a granddaughter. I'd failed as a girlfriend. I'd failed as a wife. I was failing as a mother. Nothing ever worked for me. No matter how hard I tried, what I did, or where I went, I couldn't escape failure. It followed me, it was attached to me like my skin, embedded in my DNA. I would never get away from it.

I cried for days. I don't know why it was so hard for me to bounce back from the ignorant words of a fraud, but I couldn't shake it. Tiffany and Keta tried to get me out of the house, but I wouldn't budge. Keta came and got my kids because I wasn't getting out of the bed, wouldn't eat, wouldn't answer the phone. The questions plagued me day and night. *How would I pay the rent? How would I buy food? How would I take care of my kids?* I now realize that I had put all of my eggs into the basket of my dream, but I allowed someone else to become the face of that dream. I naively allowed myself to believe that someone else would get me to my goal, that since I had endured so much already, I was owed a golden ticket.

I don't remember how long I sat in that depressed state before I decided it was time to get up, but I do remember having to call The Salvation Army and St. Vincent De Paul for help. I remember standing in lines at churches, alongside drug addicts, alcoholics and homeless families to get food boxes so I could feed my babies because I got denied food stamps. I remember interview after interview, and not getting a job. I remember going through some of the most humbling days of my life. Most of all, I remember how God kept me. How even with no job, we didn't go hungry, we didn't see the street, help consistently seemed to show up. We didn't always have what we wanted, but we never went without. When I finally got the nerve to tell my Granny and my aunt how bad it really was, of course they helped as much as they could. I learned more about myself those first few months of being in Georgia than I had my entire life, and I learned that God truly does provide.

PART FOUR:
MRS. HUDSON

Golden

Golden like the brown of his eyes
Golden like his hand on my thighs
I breathe him...
I inhale, and exhale him.
My oxygen is filtered through the dioxide of
him and without it...
I can't live.
See, I've spent endless nights on one night
stands, Countless years searching for the
perfect man, The one who could see into
me, become one with me, flow all up into
me...
But I kept coming up empty.
Til one day I said "Lord, I've exhausted my
search. My heart is on over exert, and I'm
tired of being hurt. So can You take one
second outta Your busy day, and just send a
good man, a Godly man, Oh, and please
make him a cute man...can You send him
my way?"
And so I waited. I sat at home full of
loneliness and sometimes spite, and I
waited. I turned down men night after night,
yet I still waited.
Sometimes with tears in my eyes that blurred
my sight, but I still waited, and waited, and
waited some more.
Have you ever noticed that the sky is most
clear just after a raging storm? The sun

shines a little brighter after the clouds form?
He's about 5'11 with caramel brown skin, and
eyes that glow like the sunset when the light
hits, and those lips? Hmmmm, Pablo
couldn't create enough paint to work with.
He is a work of art.
His heart is as big as Texas, and the warmth
it exudes envelopes me, and I've never seen
a single father exhibit such love and
responsibility. His laugh is so contagious it
ripples right through me. One night, he took
me to Passion in Poetry, I looked over and
the realization hit me: the Bible says it's a
good thing for HIM to find ME! And all of my
waiting was just preparation so that I would
be ready when he got to me.
Well, just over 5 months from that night of
poetry, he changed me, he completed me,
he found me, he married me! And now I'm
anxious to go back and tell them how his
touch shoots lightning through my bones.
How the tip of his tongue can do no wrong.
How the rock of his stroke is super strong,
but how most of all to him I belong...forever.
Cuz I'm not his homie-lover-friend, or his B-
U-D- D-Y. I'm not some one night stand or
meaningless moment in his life: I-AM- HIS-
WIFE~~~And in the Bible, it talks about the
MARRIAGE BED being undefiled.
So when he wraps his rippled arms around
me and looks into my eyes,

When he inhales deeply of my love and
exhales a satisfied sigh,
When he trails a line of kisses down the
curve of my spine,
I give thanks to the Most High!
Thanks for giving me the strength to end my
search and let his begin,
Thanks for teaching me how to depend on
the spirit that lives within,
Thanks for sending my angel to earth so our
lives could begin,
Thanks for showing me that love really is
Golden...
...like the brown of his eyes
Golden like his hands on my thighs
He breathes me.
He inhales, and exhales me.
His oxygen is filtered through the dioxide of
me and without it...
He can't live...

~Shaquenia Hudson - 07/29/2010~

CHAPTER 19

I had been in Georgia for a while, but I hadn't really been on any dates or met anyone. I was slightly lonely and very bored. Back home, I was used to dating, talking on the phone and getting a lot of attention from male friends and guys who wanted to be friends. Tiffany decided that it was time for me to get on the dating scene and declared that she had the perfect man for me to meet. Paul had a friend (we'll call him Ralph), that he used to work with. Ralph was divorced with two boys, a working, Christian man, and Tiffany swore that he was handsome and the sweetest guy she'd ever met. She sold him as perfect for me and showed me some pictures of him. He was cute, and she kept talking about him until I agreed to let her make the match.

Tiffany made the initial contact with Ralph via text, describing me to him, I'm sure also giving him the 'she's perfect for you' speech, and sending him pictures of me.

To the pictures he responded, *'WOW, I think she's out of my league'.*

I remember that stopping me in my tracks. I've never been the girl that thought I was super pretty or deserving of a lot of praise, so his reaction was humbling and endearing for me. He obviously wasn't some arrogant guy with a selfish attitude. I blushed, giggled a bit, and agreed that he could have my number.

Ralph and I connected from our first conversation. It was refreshing. We talked about our previous marriages, we talked about God, we talked about our children, we talked about relationships. We spent hours on the phone every night. He was respectful, funny, caring, attentive, everything that I loved in a man. He was the exact opposite of Jackson, and I assumed that's what I needed. I'd long since decided that I needed to let go of my bad boy fetish, and Ralph was far from a bad boy. He was soft and loving. We prayed together. He texted me throughout my day just to say hello. He called me 'Beautiful' as a nickname. I was enamored.

The first time that we met in person, he came to my apartment, and we agreed that I would come down to the parking lot. I didn't know him well enough to invite him in or introduce him to my children, but we had been talking on the phone so much that we had grown impatient with not seeing each other. I was so nervous waiting on him that day. I changed clothes four times. Played in my hair for an hour. Called Tiffany and Keta and told them I thought I was having an asthma attack. Stared in the mirror a million times. It was brutal.

I buzzed him into my gate and tried to play it cool walking down the stairs, but I had this huge, lopsided grin on my face. I felt like a teenager all over again, and I would have been embarrassed except when Ralph got out of the car, he had the matching grin on his face too.

"Wow. WOW! You're beautiful. You're gorgeous!"

He just kept saying it over and over, and of course, that made my already ridiculous grin even wider. We sat in that parking lot for hours that evening. I remember running in to check on the kids a couple of times, but other than that, I sat out in his car and talked and laughed and bonded with this man that I'd just physically met. It's incredible that we had so much to talk about that day because for a few weeks, we'd been talking on the phone all night, every night. By the time he left, he'd asked me on two dates for Valentine's Day weekend. I was all in.

Without knowing it, I began to recreate myself again. This time, I didn't have to become someone I wasn't, but since I still didn't know who I was, I began to create a contrived confidence. I moved like I had the answers, like I was fearless, like I was the woman I wanted to be. Down here, in this new place, no one knew my story. They didn't know my fears or my failures. I could pretend to have it all together. I could pretend like my identity was set and strong and immovable. I could make this man believe that what he thought he saw was true. *Mask On.*

A few weeks after we met, Ralph helped me through one of the hardest things I've ever experienced. My sister Keta was pregnant with twins, and she went into labor prematurely. There were all types of complications that night and beyond. The twins were born, and we almost lost both of them. They both survived, but one wasn't able to leave the hospital for five months, and when she did, she had a feeding tube and a list of other issues. The night they were born, Ralph stayed on the phone with me the entire night praying and offering encouragement. I was scared to death, worried about my sister, helping her husband and my nephews coordinate everything going on, and most of all fearful that we were going to lose a baby. I was trying to be strong for my family but inwardly petrified that I wasn't strong enough to handle it if God decided he wanted to take that baby back. Ralph was awesome that night, and in the days and nights to come. I honestly believe it is what endeared me to him in those early days.

Ralph was a breath of fresh air after I came out of a very dry place. He was a Godly man, a man with principles, a man that listened to me and didn't try to boss me around. Unlike Jackson, he asked my opinion, he didn't give it to me. He was interested in my day. If I was upset, he was concerned. We went for ice cream, and long walks under the stars. I cooked for him and he brought me flowers. He showed up with cards for no reason and started calling me his 'Detroit Boo'. Everything about Ralph was perfect, maybe too perfect.

Because things had gone so wrong with Jackson, it was very important for me to do things the right way with Ralph. We were not having sex. I called home to Granny about him, expecting her to give me the 'be careful' speech, but she told me to let him meet the kids and see what happened. I was floored by her response. I called my Detroit pastor about him, expecting to get the 'slow down' speech, but he told me 'sometimes, this is exactly how these things work'. Again, I was floored that no one was telling me that I was moving too fast.

A month or so after we met, Ralph's pastor was advising him to marry me. I hadn't found a job yet and was packing up to move out of my apartment. Tiffany and Paul invited me to move in with them again, and even offered to renovate their garage so that I could feel like I had my own space. I didn't want to move, and I definitely didn't want to live in a garage, but I felt like I'd run out of options. Ralph showed up one day and told me to unpack my boxes and marry him.

My circumstances made it a tempting offer, but I had been through too much in my life to just jump at his words. I didn't really know this man. We met in January, and it was only February. How in the world could we get married? Yes, it had been a whirlwind, and yes he seemed to be everything I was looking for, but marriage? I was very involved in my church in Georgia, and Ralph had started visiting with me sometimes. I spoke to my Pastor and First Lady, and they recommended marriage counseling. I was unsure, but I was running out of excuses not to.

Although I was still trying to find myself, there was one thing that I knew for sure. I was tired of being the 'man', handling all the responsibilities in my household, being the protector, instead of the one to be protected. I was tired of feeling the need to be hard, like I couldn't let my guard down. So many women around me were proclaiming that they didn't need a man, and maybe they didn't, but I was raised under the belief that without a man the house is out of order. My first marriage had failed, and for a long time, I wasn't sure if I'd ever want to marry again. I grew to understand that it wasn't the institution of marriage that failed, it was two people who had separate ideas of what marriage really was. I knew that I could live my life without a man, I could even take care of my children without a man if I had to, but that didn't mean that I wanted to. I wanted to be taken care of. I wanted to be a mother and a wife. I wanted to work *when* I wanted, *if* I wanted. I wanted the old-fashioned idea of marriage. I was still chasing that picket fence. I told Ralph all of this, and I was proud of myself for doing so. There was a time when I would've kept quiet and waited to see how it played out, but I let him know what I was looking for in a husband. That I was ready to take off my cargo pants and combat boots and put on my stilettos and skirts. Ralph told me that he wanted me to have whatever I wanted, and that he would show me.

Our children were getting along great. We had begun to blend our lives like couples do, with me picking up his oldest son and keeping him until Ralph got off work. He picked up his youngest son every weekend and he stayed at my house, called me Mommy, fit right in with everyone else. We took the kids out for dinner or ice cream and a movie as a family. We played games. We went to my family events. We visited both churches as a family with no issues. It all just seemed...right.

One day Ralph showed up to my house with a folder full of his important papers. Bank statements, check stubs, insurance information, social security card, birth certificate, bills, everything needed to run his life. He looked at me said,

"Just leave me enough for gas and haircuts every week. You pay everything else we need. Unpack your boxes."

Granny had always taught me that when a man wants to do something for you, you don't have to ask him, you don't have to tell him, he will just do it. In my head, this man was trying to show me that he was serious, that he wanted to be with me and take care of me and my children. He was trying to prove to me that he didn't have anything to hide, that he wanted me to be a part of his entire life. It worked.

Towards the end of February, I unpacked my boxes, and we started a six-month marriage counseling plan with my Pastor and First Lady.

CHAPTER 20

During this time, Ralph and I were continuing to get to know one another. The kids were getting closer and we were all operating like a unit. Ralph and his oldest son, Benjamin (not his real name) were staying with a cousin where he contributed to the bills and paid rent. They ate most of their meals with me, and he was also paying the bills at my apartment. When Ralph and I started dating, Ben was a mediocre middle school student, with grades that left a lot to be desired. His mother had died in childbirth, and Ralph, who had been in the army at the time, was suddenly plunged into single fatherhood. To his credit, Ralph quit the army and became a full-time dad, raising Ben primarily on his own, with help from his mother and other family.

I've always been a mother hen, so when I heard their backstory I immediately wanted to be there for Ben. I couldn't imagine him growing up without a mom. There were times when he seemed so sad, like he needed something, like he was missing something. I determined that he was missing a mommy, and I was more than willing to play that position in his life. Ben was shy at first, but opened up quickly, first to me, and then to my kids and the rest of my family. I began going to his school, meeting his teachers, implementing plans to improve his grades and behavior. It wasn't long before he was calling me mom and I considered him one of my own. Ralph and I were in awe at how well our little family was blending. We'd heard horror stories about trying to blend children from previous marriages, but we didn't seem to be having any of those problems. We felt that God was blessing us, and we were extremely grateful. Before the semester was over, Ben was on the honor roll and his teachers were singing his praises. It was an awesome turn around, and even better, Ben was smiling more. His eyes lit up when you complimented him, and he was excited to tell you about his progress. The transformation was obvious, and we felt that our prayers were being answered.

During marriage counseling, my pastor asked us a very hard question. Since I had a church home, and Ralph had a church home, which church would we choose once married? That was a difficult decision for me because although I knew that traditionally I was supposed to follow my husband, his church was weird to me. His pastor seemed very controlling whenever we visited him and his wife and something about them was unsettling to me.

In contrast, at my church, I was on the praise team, I was a choir director, I was very active in the women's ministry and the youth ministry, and I served in several other capacities in the church. I couldn't imagine leaving the place that I'd called home since leaving Detroit. Ralph was also attached to his pastor and his church and I assumed that we had hit a stalemate, but he agreed to begin worshipping with me. He slowly transitioned from his ministry to mine, and my congregation loved him. In hindsight, I realize that there wasn't much that I wanted that Ralph wouldn't do. He generally allowed my desires to take the lead in our lives. At the time, it was another endearing quality, much later, I saw that it wasn't.

The more time our families spent together and began to mold our lives together, I began to notice that Ben would have these melancholy moments. He would get quiet. Stare out of windows and want to be alone. He was twelve years old, and on some levels, it was to be expected, but because I was watching so closely for any sign of something going wrong, I think I picked up on it.

I noticed that he would get angry whenever someone complimented my daughter, which happened a lot because Arionna was a very smart girl who always excelled academically. Where Ben had to work at getting good grades, it came very easy for Arionna. I had always rewarded my children when they did well in school, and that didn't change, I just added Ben and his brother into the mix. I never made a difference between the kids, and I never allowed the kids to make differences between each other.

Whenever Arionna had good news, she'd run home to tell me, and then ask to call Granny, Aunt Madie, Aunt Mikoe and everyone else she could think of back home. They had always showered her with love, affection and encouragement, and that didn't change when we moved. I don't know for sure if this is what got to Ben, but there was a noticeable change. He no longer wanted to play with Arionna, opting to give all of his attention to RJ, who was three at the time. If the boys were playing a game and Arionna came over to play, Ben would get up and go into his room. He made it very obvious that he wanted nothing to do with her. I watched this go on for a few days, and then I mentioned it to Ralph. My concern was that this behavior was hidden resentment and would turn into violence against her when we least suspected it. I suggested therapy for Ben, and Ralph agreed, having also noticed some odd behaviors. There was a gentleman who attended the church who counseled young men and boys as his profession and after speaking with him, we scheduled a session for Ben.

Initially I expected Ben to resist counseling, to be upset with us or put up a fight, but to our surprise, he loved it. He was in sessions with other boys his age and his counselor reported back that he was receptive and responsive during group. He did point out that there were some areas that he felt Ben needed to develop, and that we were right to get them addressed now. I remember breathing a sigh of relief that we had averted a crisis. Ben didn't right away rush to be around Arionna, but he didn't keep going out of his way to be mean to her either. Progress was progress.

Ralph and I were now mid-way through our marriage counseling and planning a small wedding. We sat all the kids down one night and asked them how they'd feel about us getting married and becoming one big family. After they got done yelling and hugging and whooping for joy, we surmised that they were alright with the idea and celebrated that night with movies and junk food. Although I still had small, nagging pulls in the back of my mind, I couldn't identify them, so I pressed forward. I mean, we had the pastors involved, we were having the money talks, the kids were getting along, we were worshipping together, we weren't blinded by sex, what could I possibly be missing?

I was adamant that my grandmother had to walk me down the aisle, so we planned to get married at my church and have a small reception at a golf course near our home in Fairburn. We had begun to make arrangements, pay deposits, and coordinate so that the Detroit family and friends could travel to Georgia, when my grandmother became ill. She had been having some health challenges, but nothing too serious, until they said she would need to have her kidney removed due to a malignant tumor. This was a major surgery, and she would not be able to travel in time for the wedding. I was devastated, but I was more worried about Granny. She was my rock, and it was time for me to be hers. After speaking with Ralph, we decided to cancel the entire Georgia wedding. I did not want a wedding that Granny couldn't attend, especially since with her age and other factors, there was a chance that something else could go wrong. I called my Aunt Madie and told her our dilemma and asked her if she could pull off planning a Detroit wedding for us. As usual, she agreed with no hesitation, and just like that, the wedding plans were back on.

At this same time, Ralph and I were facing another dilemma. During one of our conversations, one day Ralph let it slip that he and Ben were sleeping on the floor in a room at his cousin's house. I was appalled. Since he'd brought me all his bills, I knew the money he was paying to stay there, and I thought that at least he had a bedroom. To find out that he was paying my bills and not even getting a good night's rest bothered me immensely, and as a mother, knowing that Ben was getting up every day going to school after sleeping uncomfortably on the floor, just pulled on my heartstrings.

It was worse when I asked if Ben could at least sleep on the couch, and Ralph told me that he was not 'allowed'. I was stunned. Who wouldn't allow a little boy without a bed to sleep on the couch to get a good night's rest? I was so angry with Ralph for not telling me this sooner. When we met, he'd explained that when he and his first wife broke up, he left everything and started over. He and Ben had their own apartment for a while, but when he got laid off from the job where he met Paul, things got hard, and he moved in with his cousin. I was no stranger to life's challenges, so I didn't judge him for that, and I saw where he had been getting himself back on his feet once he got a new job.

We were about one month from being done with counseling, but the wedding was still a few months off. I didn't know what to do, but my conscious wouldn't allow me to continue taking Ralph's money knowing how he and his baby were living. There was no easy solution. Living together was a hard choice because we were abstaining and didn't want to fall into the temptation of sex. We really were trying to do things the right way, but I didn't see any other outcome that would allow me to sleep at night. We decided that since we were so close to being done with marriage counseling, Ralph and Ben would move in with us for those last few weeks. Ralph would sleep on the couch and we bought Ben a bed to sleep in the room with RJ. We spoke to Pastor and First Lady and they agreed to marry us in the church office once we were done with counseling in July, and we would still go to Detroit to have our ceremony in September.

CHAPTER 21

Ralph and I had a simple ceremony in the Pastor's office with only the First Lady and my sister as witnesses. My sister grabbed me outside the Pastor's office.

"You sure about this?" she asked, while fixing one of the twists in my hair.

"Yea. I'm good. We're doing this. Right?"

She just stared at me, with this look she's always had. The looks says, *'who are you trying to convince, me or you?'*

"It's not too late Queenie. We can still walk back out the door. This all happened really fast. You can wait."

"I'm good. I am."

At that exact moment, I felt my mask lock into place, but I didn't understand why. I loved Ralph, he had been good to me. The kids loved him. He was providing a home for us. He was attentive to our needs. He was a Godly man. He wasn't abrasive or abusive. He had dreams and goals, and he was supportive of mine. Both of my pastors approved. I didn't have to hide him or lie about him. So what was this hesitation? Jackson was at the opposite end of this entire spectrum and I married him in a heartbeat, so why was I so unsure of a man who fit the bill in every way?

I didn't know the answers to these questions, and all of this flashed through my mind in a split second. One of the beautiful things about the relationship between Shaketa and I is that we've always been able to communicate without words. We stared at each other. My look said, *'I have no idea what I'm doing but I'm just going to keep moving forward'*. Her look said, *'I got you, no matter how this goes, even if we need a shovel and some gloves one day'*. We had shared a similar stare down on her wedding day, so the script was familiar. I nodded at my sister, she smoothed my simple black dress down, we walked into the office and I got married.

I was so nervous on the trip to Detroit. Even though Ralph and I were technically already married, most of our family and friends didn't know. Added to this was the stress that no one in my family had met Ralph yet, and my family could be brutal. I knew that I was going to get hit with all of the questions that I had pushed to the back of my mind. *Who the hell is this guy? You don't even know him! Why are you getting married so fast? Are you pregnant? Are you crazy???* I had no idea how they would react, and even though I was pretending otherwise, it really did matter to me.

It was Labor Day weekend. This was our first family trip, and although we were bummed that Ralph's younger son wasn't able to travel with us for the wedding, everyone was excited, especially Arionna and RJ who couldn't wait to see Granny and the rest of the family. Even Ben was happy and excited to finally meet the people that he had spoken to on the phone. There was still a ton of details to be taken care of, but we were all looking forward to an amazing time.

To my surprise, the weekend went off without any major glitches. There were a ton of meet and greets, dinners, a bridal shower thrown by my Sorors, windy weather when we needed sunshine, priceless time spent with my grandmother, lunch with my pastor, shopping with my dad, hair, nails, photographers that didn't show up, the typical Ileene-is-not-coming crisis, and the normal hustle and bustle that goes into the days and hours leading up to a wedding. In the end, my family did a phenomenal job pulling off a last-minute wedding, with a small budget and the bride seven hundred and fifty miles away until the very last minute.

The highlight for me was my Granny walking me down the aisle in the church that she had labored in for over fifty years. We walked arm in arm, like we'd done everything else, together. She held me up, her strength carrying me, her scent comforting me. If she had any reservations, she didn't tell me. She let me do this one thing on my own, with her support. She stood with me. It was an action so unlike her, to move in silence, and it showed me just how much she loved me. It told me that she saw me trying to grow up and was willing to allow me to do so. It also reminded me that she'd always have my back, no matter where life took me.

Surrounded by friends and family, Ralph and I exchanged vows, and then, along with the kids we poured sand into a glass vase to symbolize the blending of our families into one. It was a beautiful ceremony. When we were introduced as husband and wife, Arionna ran over to me and grabbed me around my waist, holding on for dear life. She was crying, and at first, I was alarmed.

"What's wrong Sweet Pea?" I asked her.

"I'm just happy that you're finally happy. I want you to be happy."

I looked at my beautiful baby girl, and tears welled in my eyes. She was crying hard, and I was overwhelmed with emotion that she cared so much for me. I realized that she had been worried about me, and this had given her a relief. Sometimes as parents we don't pay attention to how much our children take on our burdens. This little girl had already endured several hurdles with me, and at nine years old, she was concerned for my happiness. That was scary and amazing at the same time.

Understanding that she wasn't yet ready to let me go, I held on tight to my daughter, and we walked out of the church together, once again ready to start a new life.

CHAPTER 22

We had been back home from the wedding for two days, and we were falling back into our normal routine. The kids were back in school, Ralph and I were back to work (I had finally found a job), and life had begun to hit us over the head. We already had a letter from Friend of the Court where Ralph's ex-wife was requesting more child support, $600 more in fact. For the years since their divorce, Ralph had been consistently paying $400 per month, with the money coming directly out of his checks every week. I had worked the census earlier that year, and once that was over, I'd found a job working at a school with special needs students. I loved the job, but the pay wasn't even mediocre. I was barely contributing to our household, but every little bit helped. Needless to say, we couldn't afford to now pay $1000 monthly in child support (for one six-year-old child). Our income had been sustaining us just fine, but there was no way we could stay afloat like this.

In addition, by Wednesday of that week, I was having pain in my back that I couldn't describe. I assumed that I'd pulled a muscle, and just needed to let it work itself out, but it got worse and worse every day. By Saturday, I could barely walk, but we had a leadership meeting at church, so I got the kids squared away at home, and pressed my way. Ralph kept asking me to go the hospital, but I hated going, and was hoping that whatever it was would clear up.

Sunday morning, I woke up and slowly began to get ready for church. Arionna came into my room and sat on my bed. I noticed that she wasn't dressed for church.

"Sweet Pea, I'm already moving slow today. Why don't you have your clothes on. Please hurry up!"

"Mommy, can we just stay home today? I'll take care of you. You should just stay home. You can't even walk. Ralph and the boys can go and we can just stay here."

"Arionna I am not staying home. Will you just get dressed so we can go? Don't make me tell you again."

"Please Mommy? Just this one time? I promise I'll take care of you. I'll make your breakfast. I'll do whatever you need. Please?"

"Girl, what's wrong with you? Go get dressed and let's go!" I yelled at her.

We made it to service and Ralph and the boys sat on their usual row. Our new, perfect little family. Pastor announced from the pulpit that we had just returned from our wedding in Detroit, and the congregation exploded with applause. Even in pain, I still did praise and worship and Arionna and I took our place in the choir stand. I remember the spirit of that service was high, the congregation was up on their feet, clapping and dancing, the musicians were in rare form, and Pastor preached a rousing sermon. It was a Sunday to remember. It was a Sunday that I would never forget.

After church, like almost every other Sunday, I had a meeting with one of the ministries I worked with. When I came out of the meeting to find my family, Ralph and Arionna were sitting in the sanctuary and instantly I knew something was wrong. Her eyes were red and shifty, her body was shaking like a leaf and her breathing seemed ragged. People tell stories all the time about maternal instincts, how mothers have lifted cars off of their babies, or how they can decipher the sound of their crying child amid a crowd of hundreds. My instincts clicked on full blast. In that second, I knew why my daughter had begged to stay home. I knew that it wasn't her typical girly dramatics like I'd originally assumed. I knew that I'd missed something, and that whatever it was, my entire life was about to change.

"What's wrong?"

"Tell her what you just told me" I heard Ralph speaking, but I didn't acknowledge him, I don't even think I still saw him sitting there. I grabbed Arionna by the arm and pulled her into an empty bathroom in the back. By now, she was shaking so badly she could barely breathe.

"Breathe Sweet Pea. Just breathe. It's okay." I said, as I wrapped my arms around her.

"You're...gonna...be so...mad at me," she managed to get out between ragged breaths and sobs.

"Arionna, I've always told you that there is NOTHING that you can't tell me. I'm not mad, I promise. Whatever it is, we'll get through it. It's okay, but you have to talk to me baby. What's wrong?"

The next thing I remember is being on the floor in my Pastor's office. Somehow, I'd managed to leave out the bathroom holding onto my daughter and make it to the office before I collapsed into a ball of nerves and emotions onto the floor. Pastor and First Lady kept asking me what was wrong, but I couldn't find my words, and even had I been able to, I didn't want to repeat them. There was a piercing pain in my chest that was keeping me from taking deep breaths. The knot in my stomach was back, the one that only seemed to surface whenever I couldn't breathe while the rest of my body was in major distress, and the knot was grower larger and larger by the second. I was hyperventilating, and First Lady was trying to get me off the floor and into a chair. Pastor had left the office to find Ralph, Arionna was still shaking, and I was counting. Three, four, five times her hand wiped her tears. Fifteen, sixteen, seventeen times her knee shook under her dress. Twenty-seven, twenty-eight, twenty-nine times she bit her bottom lip. One, two, three times she asked me could we stay home...and then my mind went back to Peter, and the morning I begged Granny to stay home.

Before I share what my daughter told me in the bathroom that Sunday morning, let me first say that I share this story with her full permission. I've always taught my daughter not to live in guilt, fear or shame. Today, she is sixteen years old, and an amazing young woman that I am proud God blessed me with. I will not give all of the details because it is still my job to protect her, but I wanted to take this opportunity to say how proud of her I am for having the strength to bare a piece of herself for the world to see, and how impressed I am with how far she's come. Arionna, greatness is not only inside of you, but it is attached to you in every way. I am honored to be your mother.

That Saturday morning, I had a leadership meeting at the church. Ralph had to work, so I got the kids up and got them together before I left. The church was only about a mile from the apartment, and they knew to call me if they had any issues. Ben was twelve, almost thirteen, Arionna had just turned nine and RJ was four.

Arionna explained to me how that morning, Ben was extremely nice to her. This was unusual because although he wasn't going out of his way to be mean like before, for the most part he still avoided her and didn't really make an effort to play with her like he did RJ. She was excited that it seemed like since the wedding he wanted to be her friend. It started with them all playing games on the PS3. Arionna described Ben laughing with her, playing with her, disarming her so that she wasn't at all concerned or worried. They were siblings, playing as siblings do. She said that she was happy, that she felt like he was finally her brother too, that he liked her and wanted to be around her. Eventually, Ben turned on a video for RJ to watch, and called Arionna into the other room. She said that he started talking to her about girls at his school, and then asking her hypothetical questions, with sexually suggestive subject matter.

The only thing I knew about Ben is what Ralph told me. That his mother died in childbirth and he'd been raised by Ralph and Ralph's mother. That he'd spent time with some uncles and his maternal grandmother. That Ralph quit the military to take care of him, which I thought was admirable. I can't tell you what possessed him to ask my daughter to show him her private parts, but he did. Arionna says he asked her to drop her pants and let him see her, to which she refused. She described knowing that it was wrong, but also not wanting to anger him. I felt myself shrink, realizing that I'd passed this trait onto my daughter through the birth canal. The idea that to be loved, she had to keep everyone happy. Ben was not thwarted however and continued to push.

Arionna told me she didn't know what to do, and she didn't want him to stop being her friend, so she pulled her pants down quickly, and pulled them right back up. Ben, after returning the favor, went on to ask my daughter to do other things that she also refused. He browbeat her, pressured her, didn't let up until he got his way. Arionna described being scared to upset him, scared because I had always taught her never to allow anyone to touch her, to see her, to even speak to her in certain ways. She was confused, helpless, and had no idea what to do, so she complied. Just like I did. To this day, I thank God that Ben didn't try to penetrate my daughter, and I thank God that she told me the very next day. I don't ever want to think about what would have happened had she not felt comfortable enough to tell me.

Back in the Pastor's office, Ben was busy denying that any of it had ever happened. He gave an Academy Award winning performance, stating how happy he was to have a mother and a family, how Arionna was nasty and lying, how he would never do anything that she said. I never doubted my baby for a second, and to Ralph's credit, he stood with me. When the Pastor asked Ralph if he believed Ben, he looked at his son and told him no. At the time I thought that he was the greatest man in the world, that under that amount of pressure and pain, the fact that he stood with us was beyond phenomenal. Later, though, I found out why it was so easy.

I was lost. Since I'd become a mother, I'd prayed one main prayer:

'Lord, please, never let the things that touched me ever touch my children. I'll deal with whatever, but please save them from that pain, that confusion, that embarrassment. Please.'

God had let me down in the worst way. The fear on my daughter's face would haunt me for years afterward.

Nobody in the room believed Ben, and it was obvious. Ralph looked defeated, Ben looked caught, Arionna looked petrified, the pastors looked dumbfounded, and I was angry. Homicidal. I needed some space. I needed to hurt something. Kill something. Scream. I wanted blood, but this was a twelve-year-old boy. How in the hell do you wrap your brain around killing a little boy in the heinous ways that my mind was imagining? The pastors prayed. I didn't.

I didn't want to go home so Ralph took RJ to my sister and Arionna and I went to the hospital. I still didn't know what was wrong with my back, and I knew it would buy me some time to think and figure out my next move. Arionna was so relieved that we believed her, and she just wanted to be with me. Her breathing was back to normal, and she seemed lighter. I kept looking at her, trying to hold back the tears. How had I let this happen to her? How had I missed it? What was wrong with me? I was the victim of all victims. I'd been through this more times than I wanted anyone to know. How didn't I see this coming?

I knew something was off, but this? I knew this boy had some issues, but this? I saw that he needed some help, but this? This? THIS?

The hospital diagnosed me with a kidney infection, gave me some meds and sent me home. We went to my sister's house and I knew I had no choice but to tell her. There was no way I could make it without telling somebody. I sent Arionna in the house, but I got out of the car and just started walking. I heard Keta call my name, but I didn't stop walking or turn to the sound of her voice. A couple of minutes later, I heard her footsteps behind me.

"Baby, my legs are shorter than yours. You gotta slow down a little bit."

One of the things I love about my sister is that she gets me. She didn't ask me what happened. She didn't do the annoying thing that people usually do, incessantly asking you what's wrong and trying to force you to speak when it's obvious you can't form words. She just walked with me. It was getting dark, and the air was cooling down, yet still we walked. Eventually, I began to tell her all of it, and I broke. On some unknown street in College Park, Georgia, I fell to my knees, and I broke. I howled to the moon. I screamed at God. I cursed myself. I damned the devil. I hurt. I hurt for my daughter. I hurt for the little girl me. I hurt for all the little girls.

I hurt, and hurt, and hurt, until I was empty.

And then I hurt some more...

CHAPTER 23

The weeks and months following were some of the worse I'd ever experienced. Though I was very used to trauma, it was grueling dealing with it as a mother. There were court dates, mediations, doctor appointments, video interviews, lawyers, child services, and therapists.

There was Ralph's mother who proclaimed,

"You should've known it would happen, I did. That's not his sister. You should've never had them in the same house."

There was Ralph's pastor who said,

"Well, there's a lot Queen doesn't know, right Ralph?"

There was Ben's maternal grandmother, who said,

"Just let him stay with me. I'll take him. He's just misunderstood."

Adding to the difficulty was that I was basically dealing with it all alone. I didn't tell my family right away, I just didn't know how to face it, how to make my mouth form the words. We hadn't spoken to Jackson in over a year, and even then it was brief and left a lot to be desired. I battled with finding him to tell him this. I knew him, and I knew there would be no way to keep him from coming to Atlanta and unleashing all hell. Regardless to how he may have handled things, those were his kids, and I knew that he would kill for them, me included. I'd already gotten word about his opinion on me getting married again, and it wasn't congratulatory. Jackson was a wild card, and I didn't know how he'd play it. I knew for certain he'd go after Ben and probably Ralph by default. Could I be certain that he wouldn't also come after me? Blame me for allowing this to happen to his daughter?

More than my safety, I was concerned about the mental and emotional stability of my children. This ordeal had taken a huge toll on them, and they didn't need another blow. For their sake, I felt leaving Jackson out of it was the best decision. I'm sure I would have felt differently had he been active and in their lives, but he wasn't during that time. I knew that I would have to tell him eventually, I just needed a bit more time. I won't say this was the best or the right decision to make, but at a time when I was trying to maintain what little of my sanity I had left, it was the decision that I made. Years later I would have to beg Jackson's forgiveness for this decision, and it's perhaps one of the few regrets that I have in my life. For better or worse, he is their father, and I had no right to keep something so life altering from him. To this day, I'm not sure he believes I didn't do this out of malice, and I guess there's nothing I can do about that. I honestly did the best I could.

Ben was arrested and taken to a juvenile facility while the incident was investigated. There, he told the doctor that he'd done this before with little girls at his schools, and that he would do it again because he didn't see any wrong. The strain of going back and forth to court was taking its toll on our marriage, but Ralph and I forged ahead. Arionna was happier now that Ben was out of the house, while RJ was confused. He went from being excited to have a big brother to being confused at the loss of one. Everyone was in therapy, but I still felt as if I was in the twilight zone.

One Sunday morning a couple of months later, I was on the stage during praise & worship. I was singing the lyrics of the songs, and going through the usual motions, but my mind was elsewhere. I was staring out at the crowd, trying to remember the last time I felt normal, asking God why He had forsaken me. Asking Him to tell me why, what had I done, what didn't I do? Begging Him for understanding. When I opened my eyes again, I was on the floor of the stage. I had collapsed, all the strength drained from my body, tears streaming from my eyes, body racking with sobs, heart settled in defeat. Someone got me up, and I heard my First Lady's voice in my ear,

"Queen, stop telling God how big your problem is, and start telling the problem how big your God is!"

I knew she was right, but I just cried some more. What God would allow this for me? For my baby? What God could see me in this type of pain? The same God that I'd prayed to my entire life? The same God that I worked for? The same God that I sang for, directed choirs for, led the youth for, did

Bible Study for? Him? That God? The same God that I became a leader for? That I dragged my kids to church for? The same God that I tried to please? *That God?*

I couldn't do it anymore. I couldn't pray to a God who loved me so little that He'd allow my greatest fear to consume me, to overwhelm me, to destroy me. I didn't want any parts of Him. From that day, it was all a show for me. I did what I was used to doing, but I didn't do it from my heart. I separated myself from the girl that believed God was in control. I turned my back on Him. My heart was broken, and I didn't see how it would ever mend again.

Finally, I called home and told Auntie Madie and Granny. They both advised me to come home. I refused at first, thinking I could just plow through, but by the end of November, I'd had enough. I put my kids in the car, told Ralph we'd see him after the holiday, and we drove home for Thanksgiving.

Falling into Granny's lap has been the way I've handled every crisis in my life, and this was no different. Granny was never fond of a lot crying, and would always shush you, forcing you to get yourself back together. This time, however, she just let me fall apart. Her hand, like so many times before, was steady on my head, and I could hear her whispered prayers over me. When she didn't know what to say to you, Granny spoke to God on your behalf. She held me, wiped my tears, and prayed until I fell asleep. It was the first true rest I'd had in two months.

I awoke to the sound of Granny and the kids laughing, the television blasting, and the smell of salmon croquettes cooking. Immediately I knew that coming home was the right choice. I didn't move right away. I lay there and cherished the sounds of the people who meant more to me than anyone in this world. I wished we could go back to the days when it was all this simple. Then I remembered, it had never been simple for me.

CHAPTER 24

Going home gave me the strength I needed to head back to Atlanta and face the rest of the court dates. The problem now was we felt as if Ben had a problem and needed in-patient help, while his grandmother was fighting to allow him to come live with her. The entire process was ridiculous. Ralph was being browbeaten by his family, who felt like he was abandoning his son and taking our side, and I felt like they were about to let a sexual deviant back on the street.

In addition, a few things had been bothering me. Ben was twelve years old, not eighteen, or even sixteen. What happened to him to cause him to act out in this way? Had someone molested him? Where had this behavior come from? If he had spent the majority of his life with his father, then what was really going on? I started to watch Ralph in a way that I never had before. At first, I thought I was being paranoid. Maybe I just needed someone to blame, someone that was old enough for me to hurt, someone that I could unleash Jackson on. Maybe I was operating in my feelings and not my intellect. I no longer knew what to believe. I was hurt, angry and confused, and still looking for someone to punish.

Something that Ralph's pastor said had also been bothering me.

"There's a lot that Queen doesn't know, right Ralph?"

What didn't I know? What did he mean? Why would he say that? I had too many questions and not enough answers. Keta and I started breaking down timelines and trying to figure out anything that didn't add up. We kept coming back to the time that Ben spent away from Ralph, with his grandmother and uncles. Did something happen to him there? Ralph's mother and I never became friends. She wasn't at all interested in me or my children. Before we got married, she came into town and Ralph took us all to meet her. She ignored everyone except Ben. She barely said hello to my kids, as if they weren't even in the room. I remember Arionna asking me later why Ralph's mom didn't like her, and I decided right then that we would not be a part of her life. Any grown woman that could be cold to children had some issues, and my temper was way too unpredictable for that. Ralph barely spoke to his mom anyway. I was the one pushing him to mend their relationship, so it was no major loss.

Everything about that set up was weird, but I didn't see the woman as a child molester. I didn't know anything about the rest of the family, so I couldn't speak on that. It was all so stressful, trying to peel back the layers.

We were also still dealing with financial issues throughout all of this. The change in child support had rendered us almost helpless in our home, and all of our bills were behind. My car had already been repossessed, and we had an eviction notice. One of the worst experiences was having all the bills piled up, with shut off notices in every envelope. Ralph and I decided that we would catch everything up with our tax refund. It was the first time that we would file as married, so it was our best option. I made arrangements with the leasing office, and everyone else we owed. On the day the money was supposed to hit, it wasn't there. We were expecting $8800, and if we didn't pay the past due rent, we were going to be out on the street. My pastor worked for the IRS, and he gave me a number to call. The nice lady on the phone informed me that our taxes had been snatched for back child support. Apparently, when Ralph's ex-wife petitioned to have the support increased, it was found that the judge who ordered their divorce also ordered him to pay $1000 monthly in child support. Initially, when Friend of the Court received the order, they calculated $400 based on his income. It was later determined he should have been paying the higher amount according to the judge's order, which put him in arrears for the other $600 per month for every year since they'd been divorced.

I literally had a full-blown asthma attack. I called Granny first, who promptly told me to get myself together and breathe. Once she got done giving me the pep talk I needed, I called Ralph and told him what happened. He left work and came home. By then, I had paced a track into our carpet. Back rent was due today. I needed a car. The rest of the bills were due. Everything was over our heads. They had just taken every dime we had, but his six-year-old was sitting pretty on almost ten grand. I couldn't wrap my head around that no matter how hard I tried. Not to mention that since Ben was going to be moving with his grandmother, we had just received a letter that he'd now have to pay child support to her as well. I wasn't sure I could take another hit.

After laying all of this out for him, I looked at my husband and asked him what we were going to do. His response was simple,

"I don't know."

Then he went into our bedroom and shut the door. I didn't bother him. I understood, that like me, he needed a minute to try and process. We thought we had it all worked out, and this was a major blow. A few minutes later, I heard him crying. Gut wrenching sobs that I've never heard any man make. I went to the door and pushed it open to reveal him on the floor, prostrate, on the side of our bed. He appeared to be praying, and he was crying harder than I had earlier. I left him alone. The fact that he was crying didn't bother me outright. I was slightly alarmed at the intensity of his cry, but hey, he was a man, not a robot. I gave him space to have his moment. In my head, this was all of it, the money, Ben, the strain on our marriage, the lack of compassion from his family, it was a lot for anyone to handle. He was allowed a breakdown.

A while later, he regained his composure, went into the bathroom, washed his face, and came into the living room where I was still sitting in the shock of our day.

"So, what are we going to do? If we don't pay today, the bailiff will be here on Tuesday."

He looked at me, and breathed the loudest, deepest sigh I'd ever heard.

"I don't know Babe."

Just like that, he lost me.

I had stood by him when most women would have packed up and walked away. I didn't blame him or browbeat him. I went to every court date and stood trying to help his son get the help that he needed. His son that had violated my daughter. With all the pain, confusion, upheaval, and stress, I remained a wife to him and a mother to our children. I went on the scheduled visits with the boy who tore my life apart. I sat in meetings that discussed his wellbeing. Now the livelihood of my children was at stake and he didn't know? We were about to lose the roof over our heads, and he didn't know? I chose to stay when my family told me to come back home and *he didn't know*??

For the next forty-eight hours I waited on him to tell me the plan. I *needed* him to get us out of this. I needed him to show me that he could handle something, that he could wear the pants, that he could stand up and be the man he told me he would be when he asked me to marry him; the man I had yet to see. I needed to breathe, to not think about something, to not handle the details. I needed him to take charge.

He didn't.

With less than twenty-four hours until the bailiff would appear, I did what I'm used to doing. I made calls. I begged for help. I asked questions. I put myself out there. I figured it out. With the help of a friend from church, I found a house to move into the next day, first month free, and the landlord gave us a break on the rent for the first few months until we could get everything back in order. Ralph followed directions. He did what he was told. Maybe some women want a man that follows, but I didn't.

It was never the same for me after that. I sat with him one night and tried to tell him how I felt. I tried to explain that I was from a city where we get things done, where we're not allowed to fall apart. It's okay to cry or scream or even throw a tantrum, but then you have to get up with a plan. I told him if I was going to be the man in our relationship, then I didn't need him. I also told him that I could get every bill we had paid, but he would have to leave. He had no response. He literally looked at the ground and said nothing. Any feelings I had for him floated away in those moments.

Instantly, I thought of Jackson. That may sound crazy to some of you, but Jackson represented a certain standard to me. He wasn't a suit and tie dude, but when things got rough, he made it happen. During the years that we were together, we saw hard times, but Jackson always figured it out. He told me what to do, he didn't ask me, or expect me to come up with the plan. That held a comfort to me that I was looking for. Jackson may have been too far on the other side of controlling, but Ralph was much too soft for me. Without knowing it, I believe this is when I first began to discover who I was, what I wanted, and what I didn't want. For the first time, I understood *why* Jackson was too much for me and *why* Ralph was too little. I needed the perfect balance, someone between bad boy and holy, between strong and spiritual. Someone that didn't need to control or brutalize me, but that knew how to handle me and my strong personality. Someone that understood that I had been in the captain's chair much too long, and I wouldn't give it up to just anyone. Someone that loved God more than me, that sought after God, and followed Him in order to lead our household. Someone not so religiously fanatic that they were out of touch with real life, or more concerned with the comforts of traditionalism than they were with the truth of spirituality. Hood Holy. That's what I wanted. It's funny because I was still angry with God, called myself not on speaking terms with Him, yet I was still looking for Him.

Communication between Ralph and I quickly deteriorated after this. We no longer seemed to be able to talk to each other. We tried counseling, and though initially it was a positive experience, it didn't work for long. I grew resentful, deciding that once again I was on my own trying to hold it all together. Slowly, I was spiraling into depression, and each day it was getting harder and harder to breathe.

One morning I got up as usual and went to work. Thankfully my job was only about ten minutes from our house, because I don't remember driving at all. Somehow, I ended up in my bosses office in a total breakdown. Tears, hyperventilation, sobbing, the works. My boss, who was also my fraternity brother, shut his office door, and let me fall apart. I was known for being silly, lively and happy at work, so my outburst took him completely by surprise. He calmed me as best he could, and politely told me to go home for the day. He expressed his concern for me, walked me to my car, and told me he would call and check on me later.

When I got home, Ralph was in the shower. I had made up my mind that it was time to ask him all of the questions that had been circling my mind for the past year. I sat on the floor of our bedroom, exhausted from all of it. There was no strength left in me.

Ralph, who didn't know I was home, walked out of the bathroom in a towel, and jumped slightly when he saw me.

"Are you gay Ralph?"

"No, I'm not gay Queen." I heard his answer, but I expected...anger, or at least surprise. Some type of reaction. Most men would've slapped the hell out of me for asking them that question out of the blue. Ralph was calm, unfazed, like he had this conversation all the time.

"Well you need to tell me something. It's not adding up. Ben didn't get that way on his own. Did you molest him?"

"What? Of course not!"

"Then what the hell Ralph! What the hell is it? Why did your pastor say there's stuff that I don't know? What don't I know Ralph? WHAT DON'T I KNOW?" No longer able to contain my emotions, I scream the last part, and then take a deep breath, willing myself to calm down.

"I don't know why he said that! You know everything Queen! You do know everything! With the exception of that one incident..."

He was still talking but my brain had frozen on the last phrase.

"What incident? What are you talking about?"

"Just that when we stayed at my cousin's house, there was an incident where one of his daughter's accused Ben of touching her."

"Wait...what? You knew? YOU KNEW THIS ABOUT HIM AND NEVER TOLD ME?" I screamed.

"Well, it was just one incident, and honestly, I didn't think about it. It wasn't that big of a deal."

"You didn't think...YOU DIDN'T THINK ABOUT IT? FOR AN ENTIRE YEAR WE'VE BEEN BACK AND FORTH TO COURT! YOUR MOTHER CALLED MY BABY A LIAR! THEY POKED AND PRODDED HER! VIDEOTAPED HER! INTERVIEWED HER OVER AND OVER AGAIN! HE LIED OVER AND OVER! THEY SAID HE DIDN'T NEED HELP AND YOU KNEW THIS WAS A PATTERN OF BEHAVIOR? YOU FUCKING BASTARD, YOU KNEW?"

I grabbed my chest, instantly unable to breathe, still trying to comprehend what he just said to me.

I spun on my heels, fully intending to grab a weapon and end his life. I headed out of our bedroom and down the stairs. It's funny how God works though. The next thing I remember is being airborne. I'm not sure my feet touched a single step, but I landed on the floor below in the living room, in a full-blown asthma attack. I remember Ralph trying to help me and having just enough strength to fight him off. I also remember thinking as soon as I got off that floor, I was going to kill him.

Apparently, I blacked out, because the next thing I remember is my sister standing over me with a nebulizer and pursed lips.

"Are you trying to kill yourself?"

"He knew." I croaked around the breathing mask she held over my face, struggling in vain to get up.

"Be quiet and breathe. I know, he told me. That idiot. He's gone. I told him if he was smart he'd be gone by the time I got you off this floor." That is why I loved this chick. She knew me, much too well.

After forcing me to sit through a full treatment, Keta let me tell her the entire story. Repeating it to her, the weight of the truth hit me, and all of my anger returned. The pain from the past year returned. The fear on my daughter's face returned. How easy it was for Ralph to believe Arionna, against his own son. It all returned.

I started drinking at about two o'clock that afternoon and didn't stop. Keta had never seen me so angry and was afraid to leave me alone. She could usually get me to listen to reason, but I wouldn't hear anything she had to say. I took a chair from the kitchen and sat it outside in the middle of the driveway. I sat in that chair, with my shotgun on one side and bottles of liquor and a glass on the other. Keta called Granny, Aunt Madie, and my dad, but I wouldn't budge. She put them on speaker, and I heard them talk, but my only response was,

"If you want to help me, then come and get these kids, because I'm going to jail tonight."

I had made up my mind that when Ralph returned, I was going to shoot him and wait on the police to arrive. I didn't care about jail. I didn't care about charges. I didn't care about anything. Night fell, and Keta still couldn't persuade me to come inside. I had stopped drinking after going through two fifths and realizing that I didn't even feel drunk. Something about that scared me, that I could be filled with an intoxicating substance and not even feel it. That my anger was so strong it could absorb the effect of the alcohol. Instead, I smoked Black and Mild cigars and sat there, in the dark, willing him, almost daring him to come home. Luckily for him, and I'm sure myself as well, he didn't come back.

PART FIVE: QUEEN

THAT'S WHEN YOU PRAY

I woke up one morning and discovered I couldn't pray
Eyes overflowing with tears, head pulsating with pain
Heart so heavy that I couldn't even make my body move
Thoughts so unstable that even I was afraid of what I might do
I looked up toward Heaven, and to be honest, I rolled my eyes
"Lord, I'm not too happy right now, and since You already know,
I won't hide.
Why do You think I can take all this?
How much more do You want me to bear?
How many more tears can You watch me shed?
How many more losses do You think fair?"
Now, Cleary, you heard me say I was unstable
To speak to my God with such disrespect
But Granny always said just talk, tell Him how you feel
Course she forgot to mention He'd put me in check
"You think I don't know what you're going through?", He said.
"You think I don't know and feel your pain?
I know every molecule that makes up your existence
Not one tear you've shed has been in vain.
When the job you thanked and praised Me for
Was not the blessing it initially seemed
When there was not enough to feed your children
And the state denied your request for EBT
When your money ran out, and your bills kept running

And the note on the door said you'd soon need a place to stay
  Instead of ranting and raving, Kicking and screaming
  That, my child, is when you pray!
  When your sister had the twins
  And you were scared the girl baby wouldn't last
  When you found out your brand new husband
  Had conveniently hidden his past
  When the son you accepted and loved as your own
  Changed overnight and became a monster
  When all of the lies and all the betrayal
  Caused both of your babies to suffer
  When a cancerous tumor threatened the life of your grandmother,
  and you couldn't be there to see her face
  Instead of wasting your time feeling guilty
  My Child, THAT'S when you pray!
  When after searching for months, and the only job you could find
  Barely covers the cost of your rent
  And by the time it clears and hits your account
  More money than was in your check is already spent
  When you unlocked your front door with a smile
  So grateful to have a place to call home
  Only to find that you'd been violated
  They broke in, took your stuff, and left your window open
  When your 10 year old daughter looks you in your face
  With tears streaming from her beautiful, brown eyes
  Because her daddy won't come, he won't even call
  And she just doesn't understand why

When you sing at more funerals in 2 months
Than you have almost in a whole year
When your grandmother, who's always been the
strongest woman you know
Suddenly, and frequently bursts into tears
When your cousin came to visit last month
You were so happy to see her, at last
But the devil couldn't stand to see your smile
Cuz when you got home, they had turned off your gas
When a week ago Thursday, you curled in a ball
Tears flowing so hard, didn't think you'd get through it
Cuz your son said, "Mama, I'm trying to wash my hands,
But there's no water coming out of the faucet"
When you're so angry, SO bitter
Harboring all these emotions you can't sort
Because although you're still a newly wed
You're already headed to divorce court
You're trying your best just to keep standing
But your knees can no longer support your weight
I know it seems bad, like all is lost
But now more than ever,
THAT'S WHEN YOU PRAY!!"

~Shaquenia Hudson - Post Divorce #2~

CHAPTER 25

Over the next few months, I lived outside of myself. Ralph tried to talk to me, but whatever I had left in me evaporated that afternoon in our bedroom. I would never look at him the same again. He put me in a position where I did not protect my babies. Had I been given all the information, I would have made different decisions where the blending of our families was concerned. I would have known to put Ben into therapy sooner and exactly for what reason. Most importantly, I would have never moved him into my home knowing that he suffered with this problem and nobody had ever gotten him any help. I'm a mother, and I would have continued to be one to him, but not at the expense of my children.

Ralph and I tried to reconcile, but it was a futile effort. Ultimately, because I had married him, I wanted to be able to say that I'd done everything I could, everything I was supposed to do. I was still trying to understand who I was and how I'd ended up in an even worse situation. When I looked at him, my stomach turned in disgust. He was weak, he had failed in his very first assignment to protect us as a family, he was a liar and he had no spine. I didn't want him. He wasn't even worth killing, he was pitiful to me, and I was ashamed to carry his name. I also blamed myself for what happened to Arionna, and by default, I blamed him. I knew I was done.

He had been gone a couple of weeks, staying with a friend, and I was trying to decide what the kids and I were going to do. I was not financially able to afford our house on my own, and my sister was telling me to come and stay with her while I figured it all out. My relationship with Tiffany and Paul had all but ceased eventually because it appeared they sympathized with Ralph over me, and I couldn't stomach that, seeing as how they were *my* family. Plus, I was still adamant that I was not going to run back home defeated and face being a failure. In the meantime, I paid the house's bills like normal out of our joint account. A few days later, I found out that Ralph stopped payment on all of the bills and took me off of the account. I was flabbergasted. With no regard for how me and my children would live, he just snatched support from under us like *we* had done something to *him*.

I honestly don't remember all of our conversations or arguments from back then. What I do remember is the feeling of worthlessness, that this man could be the cause of something so heinous in our lives, and then treat us like we were nothing. I sat in my room, listening to the soulful notes of Jill Scott and Rachelle Ferrell, face in my pillow so my children wouldn't hear the screams ripping from my throat, heart beating so hard that I could feel it's pulse in my fingertips. Why did this keep happening to me? What was wrong with me? Wasn't I a good girl? Didn't I treat people right? Why did God allow all of these tragedies in my life since birth?

I was hollow inside. Numb. I didn't belong to anyone. I never would.

For a while, my motto became 'completely unstable and wildly whorish'. I was tired of being the good girl, so I became the opposite of everything I'd ever been. All my life I'd been known as the girl that tried to have morals, that refused to hop in bed with guys just because they wanted me to. I was labeled hard to get, and 'church girl'. I didn't have a long list of men I'd been with, and I was proud of that, but where had it gotten me? Two failed marriages, multiple sexual assaults, disrespected, abused, misused, lied to, hurt, disgruntled and now, numb.

So, I stopped turning men down.

There was the security guard who had been after me for months.

The cop who was ten years younger than me.

The older guy I used to supervise.

The married man who wanted to leave his wife.

Meaningless encounters that made me feel worse and worse about myself. They wanted sex. I wanted someone to hold me. Someone to make me feel loved, protected, someone to make me feel...something, anything. I didn't realize how far gone my mind was until there was a deacon sitting on my couch holding himself, offering to pay all of my bills (once he figured out how to sneak the money out of the joint account he shared with his wife), if I would just become his mistress. I put him out. That was the wakeup call.

Thankfully I had enough sense to protect myself with all of these men, and I thank God that even when we turn our backs on Him, He NEVER turns His back on us. I temporarily lost my mind, but I didn't lose my life or my health, and I know it's because God kept His hand on me. Besides Keta, I don't think anyone else knows about this destructive period in my life, how bad it got, how much of a toll the events of that year really took on me. With the help of God, writing this book gave me the strength to face it all and the wisdom to identify those feelings and behaviors I was experiencing that I didn't understand. I can share my darkest moments with no shame because I know they all worked together for my good.

It was now nearing the end of 2012, and life was a struggle. My familiar sad song was spinning: too many bills, not enough money, two children and a broken heart. Stubborn like the woman who raised me, I was determined to find my way, and so I forged ahead, looking for better paying jobs, enrolling in grad school, building a plan that might not help me in the moment, but would hopefully pay off long term.

Savannah College of Art and Design was the balm my open wounds needed. I always knew that I wanted to write, but I also knew I wasn't very good at it on a professional level. I left my first workshop in tears. The professor and other students tore my piece apart and made me feel like I belonged in an elementary school creative writing class. These were real writers, literary writers, and I did not measure up, but for the first time I was doing what I loved. I was surrounded by people that understood the effect words had on me because they also lived inside the bubble of that love. I met people from all walks of life, all ages, all stages. For the time I was on campus, I could pretend like my world didn't exist. It was a beautiful lie, and I bathed myself in its glow.

With every assignment, my writing improved, and so did my mind. As often as possible, I used the work as therapy to write about what I had been or was going through. Just like in high school, writing again saved my life. It centered me, realigned me with gravity, slowly pulled me back to earth. This was the first time I didn't wear a full mask because it was futile. They would know who I really was by the work I produced. One day I realized how happy I was just being me. Queen. The black girl with the loud mouth and mother hen personality. The woman who left her feelings on the page, raw, free, and open for the world to see, with no concern for literary structure or appropriateness. The chick who wrote exactly how she lived, tortured. Just me. An empty shell in search of filling.

Back in Detroit, Granny was having a plethora of health challenges. Battling rheumatoid arthritis had caused her to need several procedures and hospital stays. She had to have a laminectomy to widen her spinal canal and relieve some of the pain and pressure off of her legs. Once, she fell and hit her head and the doctor wanted her to stay overnight for observation and testing, but she convinced my cousin to take her home. I threw a fit. She was getting older and more stubborn and could be quite the handful if you didn't have the personality to stand up to hers. Auntie Madie and my cousin Renee had been with Granny every step of the way for all the appointments and procedures she'd needed while I was away. I was very grateful for them, but I was also feeling guilty that I wasn't there to take care of her myself. I considered Granny my responsibility. She had taken care of me basically from birth, and no one on Earth meant more to me besides my children. I had flown in a couple times to be there with her when I could, but I still worried about her terribly, and was not comfortable with her living alone anymore.

She and I were alike in so many ways. Although I asked her several times if she needed me to come home (she is the only reason I would concede to do so), her pride wouldn't let her say yes, and of course, my pride wouldn't let me accept that the plans I had for a life in Atlanta had gone terribly awry, and it was time to leave. So I was surprised when she called one day and asked,

"Do you think you would ever want to come back home?"

Granny and I were extremely close, and we spoke every single day. Her question was odd and came after we'd had a difficult conversation about her health and living situation. Besides me, Granny wouldn't even entertain the idea of living with anyone, but lately I had been trying to plant the seed that perhaps we should start looking at some assisted living facilities. She was having none of that.

"Mommy, do you want me to come home?"

"Oh no, no. I was just wondering if you ever thought about it, you know."

"If you ask me to come home, I'd come in a heartbeat. You know that."

"I don't want to interrupt your life. You have the kids and everything. I'm fine."

"Give me a couple of months. I'll be home as soon as I can Mommy."

She didn't argue, and just like that, the decision was made. Granny had always been healthy, but the last couple of years she had spent more time in the hospital than she had in her entire life. She would never admit it, but I knew her well enough to know that she was becoming afraid, the constant doctor visits, tests, hospital stays, and rehab stints were taking its toll on her. Plus, I was the only one who could stand up to her and win. I felt it was my duty to take care of her the same way that she had cared for me my entire life, and I was happy to do it. She was my blessing, now it was my turn to be hers.

Looking back, I see God's hand all over this. He always moved me when I was too stubborn to move myself. He knew there was only one person in the world that could get me to leave that dry land and He deftly played His trump card.

Two months later, all of our belongings were packed in a twenty-six-foot truck, my children were safely belted in the back of my vehicle, we hugged my sister and her family goodbye, and hopped onto I-75N, headed into a winter storm and back to the place I called home.

EPILOGUE:
THE JOURNEY BACK
TO ME

SANKOFA

"Se wo were fi na wosan kofa a yenki"

"it is not taboo to go back and fetch what you forgot."

(a word in the Twi language of Ghana, translation as stated by the University of Illinois Springfield Department of African American Studies)

*S*ankofa. Sometimes you have to go back to where it all began. I am much better able to understand the reasoning behind some of the things I've gone through just by taking the time to look back. Looking back doesn't take the pain away, and it doesn't make you forget what's happened to you, rather it provides answers to questions that have burned the inside of your heart. It allows you to see the people who have hurt you in a different light, to understand their mental makeup, and to start the slow process to forgiveness because you are no longer the only victim. Sankofa is reaching back into your past and taking only what you need to move into your future. I would rather believe that my parents didn't hurt me because they were heartless or cruel, but more because they both had underlying experiences and issues that needed addressing before they ever conceived me.

At thirty-eight years old, I was taught that I'd lived my entire life in an identity crisis. I didn't understand my value. I didn't look at myself the way God looks at me. I didn't say the things about myself that God says of me. I didn't know that I was fearfully and wonderfully made. I didn't know that the love I was searching for on the outside was residing within me because God was there all the time. I couldn't see it. I was paralyzed by my pain, and when the pain subsided, I spent the rest of my time trying to become who the world said I needed to be. I locked myself in a prison, all the while screaming to be free.

This book has been a gift from God. The process of naming my pain, of releasing myself from those things that have held me captive, of looking in the mirror and being honest about what I see, has changed me in ways I never thought possible. I'm learning to value myself, to be okay with who I am, faults and all. I'm learning that I don't have to wear the mask to be loved, because anyone that requires me to change in order to receive their love, time or devotion is not worth mine. I'm learning to be a better mother, to allow my children to flower the way God intended, to parent with less control, although that's still hard on occasion. I'm learning what self-love means, and that it's okay to be selfish with me from time to time. Most of all I'm learning that it's okay to make mistakes, that I don't have to be perfect, or live up to any human expectations of my life.

I also want to be very clear that life is still hard. It is a daily fight to keep my past in its place of submission, to keep it from creeping into my present and wreaking havoc on my future. There are days when I wake up angry, without understanding why, and until I blow up at one of my children, I don't even recognize it as destructive behavior. Countless times, I've gone to them and apologized for screaming my head off at some minor offense. I still struggle with feelings of unworthiness, finding it hard to place value on my talents, and my time, trying to understand why someone would choose me when so many people can sing, write, or speak better than I can. I struggle with my faith, knowing that God can, but wondering if He will, if I deserve it, if I've missed my chance. And yes, although I no longer chase behind it, I still long for love. I feel the pain of two failed marriages, the loneliness of my empty bed, the desire to be a wife, a help meet, a rib.

My point is, I will never understand all the why's. I still cry sometimes. I still struggle. But I no longer carry the chains. I'm no longer bound by the weight. I no longer wear the mask. I am experiencing true freedom. Part of that freedom comes from sharing the deepest parts of me with the hearts that are still trapped. I hear your cries, I feel your pain, I see your masks. I understand and I'm not judging. My story doesn't end here, this wasn't my miracle or my breakthrough. I had more tears to shed, more heartbreak to endure, more to learn, and I'm going to share that with you too.

I used to beat myself up because it took me so long to write this story. I thought it reflected some deficiency in me. I now understand that God was still giving me the words, I was still learning from my wilderness, He was still pruning me, molding me, plucking me, teaching me. Everything happens in His time, and I'm so grateful that He knew what I didn't.

It's not lost on me that this book will be released at the height of the #MeToo Movement. A time where women have shown strength, bravery, and the determination to no longer be called victims. A time where we stand united in freedom from the bondage of secrecy and shame. A time where our power comes not from some contrived notion of who the world says we need to be, but from truth, honor and sheer will. It is sad to say that in 2018 we live in a country plagued by stories of domestic abuse, sexual assault, sex trafficking and the countless brutal deaths of women and children. It is sad that we have to argue about these issues and fight for their importance in the world. It is sad that the very leaders sworn to protect us sit in offices of power and perpetuate the very evil they should be saving us from. It is sad, but it is no longer surprising.

Well square up, because no longer will we sit idly by, clothed in fear, quietly watching while you rape and murder our girls. No longer will we wear what *you've* done to *us* as badges of dishonor or shame. We are ripping off bandages, exposing your dirt, letting the trails of blood lead directly to your doorsteps, into your homes, and underneath your skins. No longer will we cover our scars with smiles that don't reach our eyes, tears that soak into pillow cases or lies we no longer believe.

We're coming out. I can say this with confidence because we've been caged too long, and the realization that you are bound is followed swiftly by the desire to be free. I asked God to show me how to use my story to help others in my position, young girls and women who are stifled by pain and unable to break free. He began to show me how most of us are bound by the same feelings of betrayal, offense, neglect, disappointment, anger, grief or emotion. The stories are endless: drug addicted, incarcerated or murdered parents; molestation; rape; violence; grandparents raising grandchildren; teen pregnancies; foster homes and juvenile detention centers; hunger and poverty; overall abuse and neglect. Children who grew up with confused ideas of love and identity, or no idea at all, and become confused adults, carrying on the cycle to yet another generation. He showed me how this happened to my parents, how it happened to me, how it started happening to my children.

In no way do I have all the answers, but what I do have is a heart that recognizes pain, and a desire to be my sister's keeper. I believe that by unveiling the wounds the world says makes us weak, we uncover the power that was always hidden within. I believe that we've worn the mask long enough, and it's time to look at our scarred, beautiful faces and fall in love with what we see. I believe that without women in our rightful places, our communities will continue to fall, our men will have no one to lead and our children won't know who God created them to be.

I believe that together, we become complete on this journey, and that true healing for us all is at the bottom of this mountain. This book brought us to the top. In part two, we will make our way back down to solid ground, and stand free from:

Betrayal

Offense

Neglect

Disobedience

Anger

Grief

Emotion

I'll see you there...

If I can help somebody as I pass along,
If I can cheer somebody with a word or song,
If I can show somebody he is trav'ling wrong,
Then my living shall not be in vain.

~Alma Irene Bazel Androzzo Thompson

SPECIAL ACKNOWLEDGEMENTS

I birthed the contents of this book the day I was born, so it is important that I thank each of you. Whether you are family, friend, acquaintance, coworker, church member, and even those I have only met in passing, I say thank you for your contribution to my story.

Dear God, it's me, Shaquenia.

Thank You for my ALL. The good and the bad. The pain and the tears. The growth and the pruning. Thank You for using my life to help others. For giving me the gift of words. For making me transparent. For giving me a heart to serve those who are just like me. Thank You for understanding me when no one else could, and for loving me when I didn't deserve Your love. And thank You for sharing Granny with me for 87 years. I know I've always said she introduced me to You, but really, it was You who gave her to me. Please honor and bless this work, that it may shine a light on Your people, and cause them to come to You.

In Jesus name I pray, Amen.

Arionna and RJ

You are and will forever remain my greatest inspiration. You made me a better woman. You taught me how to love, how to be selfless, how to look past myself and my own pain and focus on something more important. My greatest accomplishment is becoming a mother. Thank you for loving me. Thank you for being patient with me. Thank you for giving me patience (still working on that one, lol). Most of all, thank you for showing me that I am important. Keep striving for the best, and it will find you. You are the greatest parts of me. Never forget that God is INSIDE of you, and He will never fail. Mommy loves you with all that I am.

Aunt Madie

When I was a little girl, I remember crying on your shoulder (well, really on your boobs), and asking why God didn't make you my mother. I looked up to you. You saw me. You loved me when you didn't have to. You listened without judgement. You gave me the best advice in parables, told in a way that didn't make me feel like a failure. Most of all, you were there. Now as an adult, I understand that God did place you in my life as a mother. When I didn't think a mother could love me, you did. When I needed a mother to comfort me, you did. When I needed the correction that could only come from a mother, you gave it. You didn't birth me, but you birthed into me, and that means so much more. Like Granny, you loved me unconditionally, and to this day, you answer my call without hesitation. You are P31. I honor you with this work of labor. You read and reread this book countless times, and I'll never be able to repay you for your expertise, your time or your patience. Thank you for giving me a new life in words Dr. Searcy. And thank you for giving me three beautiful, talented, and loving sister/cousins to dote on for all of these years. They shine because you taught them how. I love you all.

Luvenia Renee

The most beautiful girl in the world. The girl with the diamond smile. The woman who taught me that meek and quiet are not weaknesses, but the greatest strengths. Over the years, life has dealt you some difficult hands. I've watched you overcome them all with grace, beauty, and virtue. I look up to you in ways I've never spoken of. You too, my love, are P31, and that amazes me. I still strive to get there, but I'm grateful that I have you as a shining example. I love you my cousin, and I always will.

The Uncles

All of you are gone now, but I will never forget. I had a special relationship with each of you. My uncles were my daddies, and I've always been proud to say that. RIParadise Uncle A.B., Uncle Charles and Uncle Marion. Take care of Granny.

The Cousins

I have always longed for a family. The picket fence, a husband, a couple of kids and a dog. Barbecues and picnics. Birthdays and get togethers. I didn't realize that all these years I've been longing for what I already had. You guys mean the world to me. Every time you show up for my contrived reasons to cook and spend time with you, you bring me joy. Every time you call just to check on me, you bring me joy. Every time you stop by just to have a drink, you bring me joy. I never realized I was this loved, and I'm sorry for that. Thank you just for being there. Even in our mess, we're a FAMILY, and that will NEVER change! Irving/Searcy Clan, I love you.

The BFs

Chelsea and Erna, for almost thirty years, you two have been my backbone. We've grown up, grown apart, come back together, survived births, deaths, tragedies, accomplishments, heartaches and failures. And we did it all together. You made me relevant. You gave me something I never thought I'd have: true friendship. You've never turned your back on me, never judged my foolish mistakes, and are always ready with a shovel and a getaway car if need be. You've fought for me, with me, and about me. Your families are mine, and mine is yours. Granny always said that a person is lucky if they get one true friend in life. Well God must really love me, because he gave me two. My friends, my sisters...for life. I love you.

Keta

You are only in a separate category because you came almost ten years later, but not because I love you any less. You showed up like a wrecking ball and just shut it all down, lol. During the times when Cee Cee and Erna and I were apart living our lives, you were there. You've cried with me, laughed with me, and tried to kill people about me (true story, lol). You were the single most irritating person during my first pregnancy, ROTF, and it was impossible to get rid of you. You have angered me, irritated me, and made me pull my hair out. But you have loved me and devoted yourself to me in a way that most never will. You are one of the strongest women I've met, and each day I'm amazed at how you make it through. God didn't give me a sister because He knew you were coming, and it wouldn't be enough room for two. You got me through one of the most trying times of my life. You helped get my children through. You were selfless. You believe in my gifts more than I do sometimes, and you have never stopped pushing me forward. You've been my pit bull since the day that we met, and I wouldn't have it any other way. I love you Sissy.

Auntie Mikoe

You taught me how to be a lady. You told me I was beautiful when I KNOW I looked a mess, lol. That's because in your eyes, I am always beautiful. I am your baby, and I know that. I love you more than I can say on this page. I feel like I hurt you when I was younger, and I hope you know that it was unintentional. In my selfishness as a teenager, in trying to find myself, living in my own head, maybe I made you feel unloved, unimportant, or removed from me. For this, I'm so sorry. I feel like the trajectory of our relationship changed back then, and we've never really recovered. I know that you love me like I'm your own daughter. I know that my children mean the world to you. I know that seeing me hurt or in pain cuts you like a knife. Please understand that I haven't always understood the ups and downs of my life, or why I reacted to them in certain ways, but I never meant to hurt you. I never meant for you to feel like you had limited importance to me. I was trying to find my way. I didn't always understand you because your life was so removed from mine. I wanted to BE you, and maybe there was a subconscious jealousy that even I was unaware of. You had my picket fence. You had my family. You had my dream. Can we get a do over??

Pastor Steven Danner

What can I say? You met me at my lowest point. I was in a black hole, and not sure I wanted to keep going. God sent you to me that day less than 30 minutes after I'd prayed for help. I KNOW that He sent you to me, and I'm ever grateful. For over a year, you poured into me, you listened to me, you fussed at me, and you gave me what the Word said. For over a year you mentored me and 'loved on me'. For over a year you pulled me back to my feet and reminded me who I am...in God. Now as my Pastor, you continue to pour into me, to teach me, to show me things I've never seen and never understood in the Word. You accept me as I am, while pushing me to be greater. I thank God for your anointing, and for allowing you to share it with me. I can now say what God says about me, and His words are the only words that matter. I love you and I'm honored to have a place in this ministry. Keep hope alive.

House of Refuge Ministries

The place where truth and love abide. It's hard to remember a time when you weren't there. From day one, you welcomed and loved me and my children. You've prayed with and for me. You've cried with me, praised with me, laughed with me, and learned with me. We've grown together, and there is much work to do. Thank you for your encouragement, for keeping my family lifted and for accepting me as I am. Let's walk this walk of humility together. I love you all.

Apostles Daren and Valerie Phillips and CUCI

I'm still amazed at how God works. The first time I came to CUCI, I had no idea that experience would last a lifetime. I was born again in that place. I experienced God in that place. My life was changed in that place. Years later, I am still gaining understanding, still looking back to that day, still in awe. I know that I have a home there, and that means the world to me. Continue to stand in the gap for others. Continue to preach the unfiltered word. Continue to open your arms and welcome the masses. Continue to let God use you to influence the nations. I love you and I'm always here for whatever you need. Thank you. I will always come back.

Pastors Melvin and J.T. Ware and MOBC

You made Georgia home for me. I walked into your sanctuary and instantly knew it's where I should be. You fed me when I was hungry. You counseled me when I was weak. Your prayers, your love, and your guidance helped me during one of the most trying times of my life. I am forever grateful. Although I'm not there physically, you are never far from my heart or my prayers. I love you all and I'll see you real soon.

Pastor Tom Bader and Chippewa Valley COG

Thirteen years ago, God brought you into my life. I had no idea when I showed up at WB20 to be your intern that you would have such a major impact on me. You saw my natural talent and allowed me to use it each and every day, and for that, I'm grateful. More so, you saw my God-given spirit at a time when I didn't recognize it. You called me out on who I am in God. He used you to remind me that I belonged to Him, that He was there, orchestrating my every step. Today, just like back then, you support me in everything I do. You offer words of encouragement, you pray for me and my children, and for my spiritual gifts. I love you, your family and the church. I am in awe of the work you do, and so humbled every time you call on me to be a part of it. Keep on listening to His voice, for his plans for you are great! *(Jeremiah 29:11)*

Pastor Patrick O. Lindsey and GBMBC

My foundation. My family. I can never forget where I come from. You've always been there for me, and I know you always will. I think of you, and I think of Granny, who sacrificed everything to keep that ministry afloat. Who believed in you and your greatness more than anyone else. Who loved you with her entire heart. I think of these things and it fills my heart. I know that you don't always understand me, but please know that I haven't strayed. I am who God made me, and I learned a lot of that in your Sunday schools and Bible studies, in your revivals and spiritual enrichment weeks. I thank you for loving me, for loving my grandmother and my family, and for giving me the foundation that I needed to build upon. I love you and I'm never far from home.

Sandra Ranger - MY BOO

When Granny was sick, you were there. When I was sick, you were there. When my kids needed you, you were there. When Granny died, you were there. When I needed a place to stay, you were there. Whenever we call, you are there, over and over and over again. I don't know what I've done to deserve your love and devotion to me and my family, but I am SO grateful that God gave you to me. You are my BOO, my partner in crime, my Lone Ranger. There are billions of people on this planet, but not many blessed with your heart, your loyalty or your grace. We have stuck by each other through thick and thin all these years, and you better believe we ain't going nowhere now! I love you Ranger. Thank you for always giving so unselfishly of your time and your heart to this little eastside girl with the big mouth. I GOT YOU BOO!

Mary B

We've been through a lot in these years. I am grateful to God that we were able to move past the trials and tribulations and remember what bonded us together in the first place. You have always been my baby, and yea, I know I tried to boss you around sometimes. (Ok, all the time, lol) I've always only wanted the best for you, and to make sure that the people around you gave you what you deserve at all times. I will always be protective, and always ready to jump in the fire with and for you. I will always be here for you. And yep, I'll probably always try to boss you (I just can't help it, teeheehee), but I understand that you're a GAW and I gotta let you live. Thank you for loving me, my children, and my family. Thank you for answering every time I call. Zeta bonded us together, but love made us sisters. 2/4thz. My Deuce forever. Love you.

Rahsaan

At a young age, you taught me that I could be loved outside of my family. You called me beautiful. You were protective and gave yourself to me fully at a time when most would think we were too young to understand. But we did. Our connection was infallible. Our souls connected. I now understand that God brought you to me at that time because I needed you. I needed someone to show me love. I needed to know that I was lovable. Thank you. For always being there, for loving me against the odds, for allowing me to hurt you even now by not giving you what you need. Thank you for seeing into my soul and loving me anyway. SM4L. 143.

Esha Efe

Some things are just meant to be, and our friendship, our sisterhood, our bond is meant to be. For every encouraging word, thank you. For listening to me cry and vent, thank you. For taking every single one of my negative statements and turning them into positive proclamations, thank you. For believing in me, and not allowing me to give up on the little girl inside, thank you. Your gifts are amazing, and I'm honored for your art to grace the cover of this story that means so much to me. I love you. The grind continues. Peace and Blessings.

Renee Bisby

I still can't believe you're gone. I'll never be able to tell you how much you impacted my life. How the lessons you taught have carried me from state to state and job to job. How you allowed me to be me, and never looked down on me for it. I'll never forget that first golf trip. Me in my denim jacket and jeans with the rhinestones across the back and butt, lol. Everyone looking at me crazy (Ed Patrick-insider LOL), while you included me in EVERYTHING, and introduced me to EVERYONE. You weren't embarrassed by me, and you never allowed anyone to treat me badly. You didn't leave me behind the next time, you just took me to buy golf shoes and a proper outfit! This is who you were, not just to me, but to everyone you met. You were there for me in all the years after I left the company. I will never forget you Bizzie. Gone too soon.

Dad

Ours is a long and ever evolving narrative. I know that I could've written you off, wiped you out of my life and moved on without anyone questioning my decision. You confused me, betrayed me, put me in an impossible position. Most will never be able to understand, and that's okay. They don't have to. I want to thank you. Thank you for always owning it. For never placing blame in the places that, honestly, would have made sense. For sitting in that dog house for as long as I needed you to. In my heart I know that your healing never would've come had it not been for the repairing of our relationship, had I not started to ask the hard questions. I'm proud of you for not letting this define you, and for understanding, even now, when I need my space. Thank you for being an awesome grandfather to my children. I know this book can't be easy for you, and when I came to you with it, your words to me were 'It's not about me. This is for you, for your healing, for your growth'. You will never know how much those words meant to me. Thank you for allowing me to do this my way. Love you.

Mom

You have taught me more than you know. Your life showed me who not to be, what not to do, what choices to avoid. Please don't see this as a bad thing, it's not. Had it not been for you, I would've had to learn from experience. I honor you as the woman who gave me birth. You may not believe it, but I love you. I care about what happens to you. I worry about you even when I don't want to. I know that I seem harsh and mean sometimes, but it's just the defense mechanism that I created to protect my heart. I believe that you love me. I also believe that one day we can have a better relationship than we do now. I'm open to that. It's been hard for us, and maybe it always will be. But that doesn't mean that we can't have love and respect. I don't need you to make up for the past. I just need you to want us to have a better future. I believe in you more than you know. Now you just need to believe in yourself. I love you. We're gonna be okay.

And for all the men and women who will read these words, I love you. I honor you. I share my story with you and hope you can find bits and pieces of your own. I am SO proud of how far you've come but know that this is just the beginning. Remember to love God first, and everything else will fall into place. Never worry about what others think and say, own who you are, and then decide where you want to be.

Release Yourself.

66922877R00135

Made in the USA
Middletown, DE
18 March 2018